Data Rookies:
Introduction to Data Analytics

Key Concepts for Beginners

Published by
Data Analytics Curriculum
https://www.dataanalyticscurriculum.com

Supplements and Companion Books

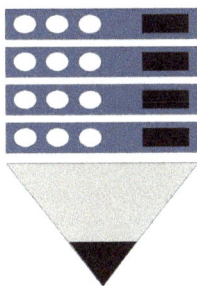

Data Analytics Curriculum

Data Analytics Curriculum, LLC creates approachable, visually engaging educational materials that make data science and AI concepts accessible to learners from high school through college, as well as independent learners.

Our core textbooks—like this one—are sold separately from lab and exercise books so they can be paired with a variety of technologies.

This book is supported by companion lab exercise books for both R (coding-focused) and Orange (no-code), with additional technology options planned for the future.

For more titles, lab books, solution guides, slide decks, and other teaching and learning resources, please visit our store or website:

Website: https://www.dataanalyticscurriculum.com

Contents

Contents

Chapter 1

Introduction

1-1 Defining Data Analytics

Learning Outcomes

1-1-1 Define data analytics and its role in decision-making.

1-1-2 Compare traditional vs data-driven decision making.

1-1-3 Distinguish between data science, data analytics, and data engineering.

1-1-4 Identify responsibilities of data scientists, data analysts, and data engineers.

1-1-5 Explain how machine learning and AI enhance data decision making.

Data analytics is the process of examining, transforming, and interpreting data to uncover patterns, trends, and insights that support decision-making. It involves techniques from statistics, mathematics, and computer science to process structured and unstructured data. Data analytics typically involves analyzing historical data to help businesses understand their past performance and make informed decisions about the future. The process of data analytics begins with collecting data and culminates in the use of data in decision making. Data analytics is widely used in business, healthcare, finance, and many other fields to optimize performance, improve efficiency, and drive strategic decisions.

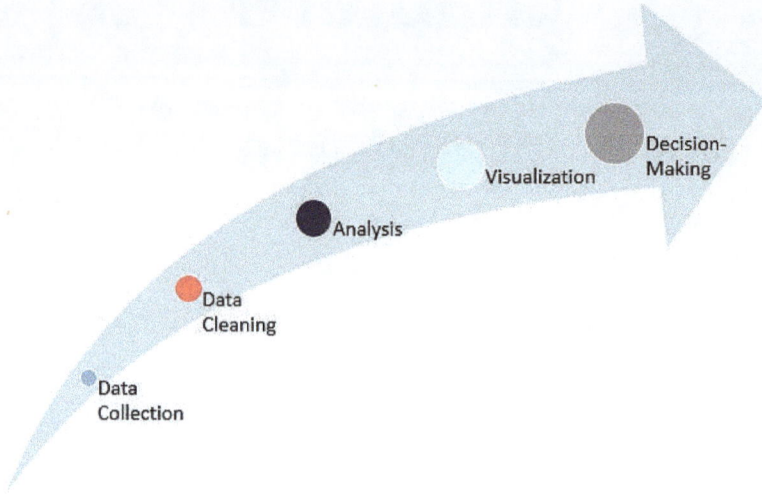

Modern Decision-Making

In today's fast-paced business world, data plays a crucial role in how decisions are made. Organizations of all sizes now rely on data to guide their strategies, improve efficiency, and make choices with greater confidence. Whether it's a small startup or a global corporation, companies are using data to streamline operations, understand their customers better, predict trends, and support long-term planning.

In the past, many business decisions were made based on gut instinct, personal experience, or limited information. That's changed with the rise of advanced analytics and machine learning. These tools allow businesses to draw insights from massive amounts of real-time data. For instance, retail companies study customer habits to fine-tune pricing and manage inventory more effectively. Supply chain managers use forecasts to plan production and avoid shortages or excess stock. In marketing, teams rely on detailed customer data to craft messages that speak directly to specific groups of consumers.

Traditional Decision-Making	Data-Driven Decision-Making
• Intuition-based	• Data-based insights
• Relies on personal experience and judgment	• Uses big data and analytics tools
• Limited data sources	• More accurate and consistent
• Less consistent results	• Data-driven predictions and trends

As artificial intelligence continues to evolve, machine learning and deep learning are reshaping how decisions are made across industries. These technologies allow organizations to work with massive volumes of both structured and unstructured data in ways that are faster and more precise than older methods. For example, machine learning can uncover trends in customer behavior, helping companies refine their products and adjust sales strategies in advance. Deep learning, which draws inspiration from how the human brain works, is especially useful in tasks like interpreting images or understanding language—areas that were once tough to analyze.

By incorporating these tools, companies can streamline decision-making, boost efficiency, and stay ahead of the competition. Looking at both past

3

and present data allows businesses to respond more effectively to new challenges and base their strategies on solid evidence, increasing their chances of success.

> **Example**
>
> Olivia Carter, a senior analyst at a national retail chain, uses data analytics to optimize inventory and pricing strategies, aiming to boost revenue and customer satisfaction. Previously, the company relied on sales data and managers' intuition, which led to issues like overstocking slow-moving products and running out of popular items, resulting in lost revenue.
>
> By implementing predictive analytics, Olivia's team analyzes customer trends, social media sentiment, real-time inventory, and competitor pricing. This data helps them predict product demand, adjust pricing dynamically, and improve supply chain efficiency. As a result, the company sees a 15products, and better customer satisfaction with products in stock at competitive prices.

Related Fields

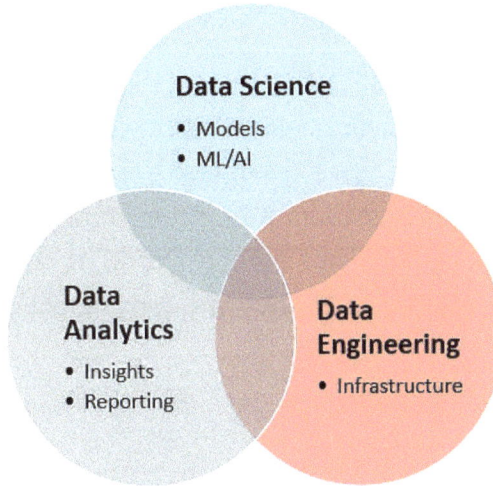

While data science, data analytics, and data engineering are all crucial components of the data ecosystem, each plays a distinct role. Understanding these differences is essential for organizations looking to deploy effective data strategies and build the right teams to drive insights and innovation.

Data Science

Data science is the broadest and most advanced field within the data ecosystem. It combines programming, statistical analysis, and machine learning techniques to build models that can predict future outcomes or uncover hidden patterns in large datasets. Data scientists typically work with vast amounts of data from various sources, applying algorithms and complex mathematical models to generate insights that support strategic decisions.

A data scientist's role goes beyond simply analyzing data; they are tasked with creating predictive models that forecast future trends or behaviors.

This might involve training machine learning algorithms on historical data to predict customer churn, sales forecasts, or financial market trends. The use of deep learning models, which simulate the workings of the human brain, is increasingly common in fields such as image recognition and natural language processing (NLP).

In addition to their technical skills, data scientists must have strong problem-solving abilities, as they often need to design innovative approaches to data challenges and adapt their models as new data comes in. Programming languages like Python and R, as well as familiarity with machine learning frameworks such as TensorFlow or Scikit-learn, are essential tools for data scientists.

Data Analytics

Data analytics focuses on analyzing historical and current data to uncover trends, draw conclusions, and provide insights that inform decision-making. Unlike data science, which is centered on prediction, data analytics tends to be more concerned with understanding what has happened and why it happened. This role is essential for organizations that need to analyze past performance to improve future outcomes.

Data analysts typically use tools like Excel, Tableau, Power BI, and SQL to clean, organize, and visualize data in a way that is easy to interpret. Their work involves tasks like trend analysis, identifying anomalies, and generating reports that highlight key insights for business stakeholders. For example, a data analyst in the marketing department might analyze past marketing campaign data to determine which strategies were most effective, helping to guide future campaigns.

While data analytics also uses statistical analysis, it lacks the complexity and predictive capabilities found in data science. However, analysts are still expected to have strong technical skills, particularly in SQL for querying databases and in data visualization tools for presenting findings.

Data Engineering

Data engineering is the foundation that supports both data science and data analytics and falls most toward computer science. Data engineers are responsible for building and maintaining systems that collect, store, and process large volumes of data. They create data pipelines that ensure data flows smoothly from various sources, such as websites, applications, and sensors, into databases or data warehouses, where it can be accessed by data scientists and analysts.

A key responsibility of data engineers is to ensure that the data is clean, accurate, and structured in a way that makes it easy to analyze. This involves handling tasks such as data wrangling, which includes removing duplicates, correcting errors, and filling in missing values. Data engineers also work with technologies like Hadoop, Spark, and cloud services (e.g., AWS, Azure) to manage big data environments.

Data engineering requires a solid understanding of databases, programming languages like Python and Java, and distributed computing. Data engineers must ensure that the data infrastructure is scalable and capable of handling the growing data needs of the organization.

Example

Trendy Mart, an online retail company, uses a data-driven strategy to enhance customer experience and boost sales, with each data role playing a crucial part.

Sophia, a data engineer, builds data pipelines to collect and organize data from various sources, ensuring it's stored accurately in a central warehouse. Daniel, a data analyst, uses this data to identify sales trends and customer behavior, helping create promotions like bundling jackets with gloves. Emma, a data scientist, takes these insights further by predicting future demand and customer churn using machine learning models and creating personalized product recommendations.

As a result, Trendy Mart sees a 20reduction in customer churn, and more efficient data infrastructure, enabling faster insights and better decision-making. This scenario shows how data engineers, analysts, and scientists work together to drive business success.

Review Questions

1. What is the main difference between data science and data analytics?
2. How has data changed decision-making in businesses?
3. What role do data scientists play in the data ecosystem?
4. How do data analysts contribute to decision-making?
5. What are the primary responsibilities of data engineers?

1-2. Careers and Opportunities

Learning Outcomes

1-2-1 Identify various career opportunities in data analytics.

1-2-2 Describe the key responsibilities associated with major data analytics roles.

1-2-3 Recognize essential technical and soft skills needed in data analytics.

1-2-4 Explain how data analytics is used in industries.

1-2-5 Discuss emerging career paths in data science.

This section explores the various career opportunities in data analytics, the industry applications driving demand, the responsibilities associated with key roles, the skills required to excel, and the future career prospects in this field.

Industry Applications

Data science and analytics are integral to every industry today. Organizations in diverse sectors use data-driven insights to improve processes, reduce costs, and innovate new products and services. Below are some key industries where data analytics plays a pivotal role:

Healthcare

In healthcare, data science and artificial intelligence are playing an increasingly important role in improving outcomes and efficiency. These technologies are used to forecast disease outbreaks, enhance patient care, and make hospital operations more effective. Predictive models can identify potential patient needs in advance, while AI tools assist doctors by analyzing medical images and other diagnostic information, supporting more accurate and timely clinical decisions.

Example

St. John's Medical Center uses AI and data science to enhance patient care and streamline hospital operations. Dr. Emily Carter, a public health data scientist, analyzes real-time data to predict disease outbreaks, such as the flu, by tracking patient symptoms and environmental factors. By detecting early signs, the hospital can alert health authorities to prepare resources in advance, reducing the impact of outbreaks.

John, a radiologist, uses AI-powered imaging systems to detect abnormalities in X-rays and MRIs, improving early cancer detection by reducing diagnosis time by 50administrator, leverages AI-driven predictive analytics to forecast patient admission rates and optimize staff scheduling, ensuring efficient resource allocation and reducing overcrowding.

In this example, AI and data science improve early diagnosis, operational efficiency, and outbreak management, leading to better patient care and more effective hospital management.

Finance

The financial industry relies heavily on data analytics for various applications, such as fraud detection, algorithmic trading, and risk management. Machine learning models can analyze transaction data to identify suspicious activities, while predictive models help financial institutions make better investment decisions and mitigate risks.

> **Example**
>
> Global Bank, a multinational financial institution, uses AI and data science to improve fraud detection, optimize trading, and manage financial risks. The bank's AI system analyzes millions of transactions in real-time to spot fraudulent activity, reducing fraud by 30pattern recognition and continuous learning. This system flags suspicious transactions for review or automatic blocking.
>
> In trading, AI-powered algorithms help the bank capitalize on market trends and stock price fluctuations by executing trades in milliseconds, enhancing profits and reducing human error. Additionally, predictive analytics in risk management allows the bank to assess loan default risks and set interest rates, accordingly, minimizing bad loans and improving profitability.

Retail and E-Commerce

Data analytics in retail and e-commerce enables businesses to optimize inventory management, forecast demand, segment customers, and personalize marketing strategies. By analyzing customer behavior and purchasing patterns, companies can improve customer satisfaction and boost sales.

> **Example**
>
> Fashion Trend, an online fashion retailer, uses data analytics to improve inventory management, customer segmentation, and personalized marketing. By analyzing historical sales data and tracking real-time inventory, the company predicts demand, reduces stock on slow-moving items, and cuts inventory costs by 20always available.
>
> Marketing efforts are also enhanced through customer segmentation. The marketing team tailors campaigns based on customer behavior, offering loyalty discounts to repeat buyers and incentives to new customers, resulting in a 30Additionally, personalized shopping experiences, including product recommendations and dynamic pricing strategies, lead to a 25improvement in customer retention.
>
> Data analytics helps Fashion Trend reduce costs, increase sales, and deliver a more personalized and engaging shopping experience.

Manufacturing

In manufacturing, data analytics is used for predictive maintenance, quality control, and supply chain optimization. By analyzing machine data and sensor readings, manufacturers can predict when equipment is likely to fail, ensuring better up time and reducing operational costs.

Example

SteelWorks Manufacturing, a steel production plant, uses data analytics to improve machine uptime, product quality, and supply chain efficiency. By collecting data from sensors on machines, the company can predict when equipment might fail, allowing the maintenance team to perform repairs before issues occur, reducing downtime and costs. This predictive maintenance ensures smoother operations and better resource management.

Quality control is also enhanced through data analytics. By analyzing sensor data in real-time, the quality control team can monitor production processes and adjust parameters when defects, like inconsistencies in thickness, are detected. This helps maintain product quality, reduce rework, and improve customer satisfaction. Additionally, the supply chain is optimized by using historical demand data and machine learning to forecast raw material needs and streamline inventory management, leading to cost savings and faster response times to customer orders.

SteelWorks Manufacturing uses data analytics to reduce operational costs, improve product quality, and enhance supply chain efficiency, enabling the plant to meet production targets and customer demand while minimizing waste.

Marketing and Advertising

Data analytics in marketing and advertising enables businesses to analyze consumer behavior, optimize campaigns, and improve targeting. By leveraging big data and customer insights, companies can create more personalized advertising strategies, leading to higher engagement and better returns on investment.

> **Example**
>
> TrendyWear, a retail clothing brand, used data analytics to improve its marketing and advertising strategies. By collecting and integrating data from various sources like website analytics, social media, and customer purchase history, the company gained a comprehensive view of customer behavior. They then used machine learning to segment their customers based on preferences and shopping habits, allowing for more personalized marketing efforts.
>
> With insights from these segments, TrendyWear created targeted ad campaigns, personalized email marketing, and dynamic website content tailored to specific customer groups. Additionally, predictive analytics helped forecast sales trends and optimize campaign effectiveness, ensuring a higher return on investment. As a result, the brand saw improved customer engagement, increased sales, and a more efficient use of marketing resources.

Additional Key Job Roles

With the growing importance of data-driven decision-making, additional key roles have emerged within the field of data analytics. These include:

Machine Learning Engineer

Machine learning engineers focus on designing, developing, and deploying machine learning models into production environments. They work with data scientists to translate algorithms into scalable solutions. Their expertise includes deep learning frameworks like TensorFlow and PyTorch, as well as cloud platforms and infrastructure.

Business Intelligence (BI) Analyst

BI analysts use data to inform business strategies and decisions, often creating visual dashboards and reports. They work with tools like Tableau and Power BI to turn complex data into actionable insights, helping stakeholders understand performance metrics and make informed decisions. This role typically does not require as much technical skill or programming as other data roles and often uses more soft skills such as good communication.

Required Skills and Competencies

Professionals in data analytics need a combination of technical expertise and soft skills to succeed in their roles. As organizations adopt more advanced technologies like machine learning, big data, and AI, the required skill set continues to evolve. Here are some essential skills for data analytics professionals:

Technical Skills

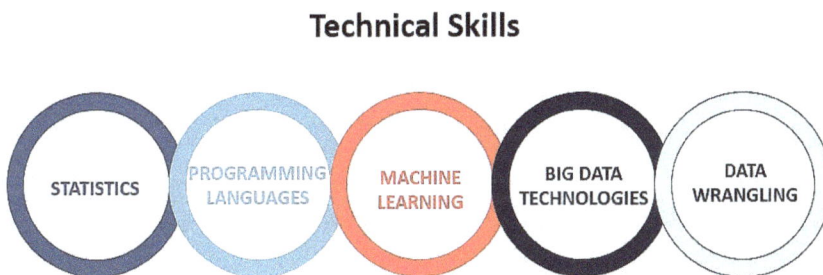

Technical Skills

STATISTICS   PROGRAMMING LANGUAGES   MACHINE LEARNING   BIG DATA TECHNOLOGIES   DATA WRANGLING

Statistics   For roles in data analytics knowledge of basic statistics is essential however further advanced math is likely unnecessary. For data science roles it may be required to study math including calculus and linear algebra.

Programming Languages   To work effectively in data science and analytics, it's essential to have strong skills in programming languages like Python, R, and SQL. Python is especially popular because of its wide range of libraries— such as Pandas, NumPy, and Scikit-learn—that make tasks like data analysis, machine learning, and visualization more efficient. R is still widely used in academic and research settings, particularly for in-depth statistical analysis, thanks to its rich selection of specialized packages. SQL remains a core tool for handling large datasets stored in relational databases, making it possible to retrieve and organize data with accuracy and speed.

Machine Learning Frameworks   For more advanced positions in data science, it's important to have a strong grasp of machine learning frameworks like TensorFlow, Keras, and Scikit-learn. TensorFlow and Keras are commonly used for deep learning projects, offering powerful tools to build and train neural networks for tasks like image recognition, language processing, and reinforcement learning. Scikit-learn is another key tool, known for its simplicity and efficiency in handling a broad range of algorithms—including classification, regression, clustering, and dimensionality reduction. Being skilled in these frameworks allows data scientists to develop models that learn from data and generate accurate predictions in practical, real-world applications.

Big Data Technologies   As companies deal with growing amounts of data, knowledge of big data technologies like Hadoop and Spark has become increasingly important for data engineering roles. Hadoop is an open-source system that enables large datasets to be stored and processed across multiple machines, making it easier to manage distributed data. Spark, known for its speed and flexibility, is widely used for real-time data processing and supports advanced analytics tasks, including machine learning and graph analysis. Cloud platforms such as AWS and Azure also play a key role, offering scalable tools and infrastructure to store, process, and analyze big data. Being familiar with these technologies equips professionals to handle complex, large-scale data challenges that traditional tools can't manage effectively.

Data Wrangling and Preprocessing   Data wrangling—the process of cleaning and preparing raw data for analysis—is a vital skill for anyone working in data science or analytics. Before any meaningful analysis or modeling can happen, the data needs to be accurate, consistent, and well-structured. This often involves dealing with missing values, removing outliers or noise, transforming variables, and combining multiple datasets. Tools like Pandas in Python and dplyr in R make these tasks more manageable, offering user-friendly functions for reshaping, summarizing, and cleaning data. Being proficient in data wrangling helps professionals ensure that the data they work with is reliable, setting the foundation for accurate and insightful analysis.

Soft Skills

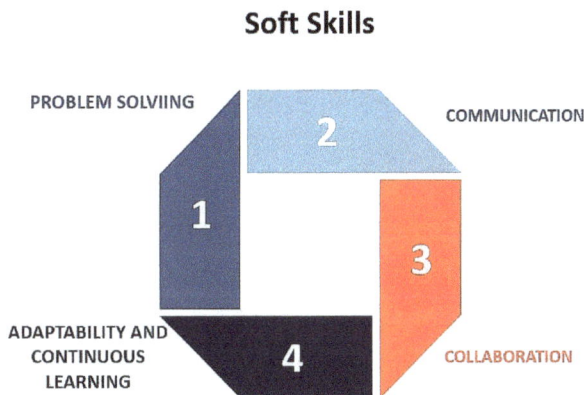

Problem-Solving   Being able to break down complex problems and develop data-driven solutions is one of the most important skills for anyone in a data-related role. Analysts and data scientists often face messy, incomplete, or unclear information, so critical and creative thinking is essential. Problem-solving in this context isn't just about spotting trends—it involves asking the right questions, choosing suitable methods for analysis, and adjusting strategies based on what the data reveals. This ability is key to everything from resolving technical issues to identifying new opportunities for improving business operations. Strong problem-solving skills allow data professionals to uncover meaningful insights that support better decisions and help organizations tackle real-world challenges.

Communication   In data-focused roles, the ability to clearly communicate complex findings is just as important as analyzing the data itself. While data scientists and analysts are skilled at uncovering insights, their impact is limited unless they can explain those insights in a way that others can understand and act on. This often means turning raw numbers into visuals—such as charts, graphs, or dashboards—that highlight key trends and patterns. Just as important is the ability to write and speak clearly about what the data shows, why it matters, and what actions should follow. Whether sharing results with executives, working alongside technical teams, or speaking to a general audience, strong communication helps ensure that data leads to real, informed decisions.

Collaboration   Data analytics is rarely a solo effort. It often requires close collaboration with people from different areas of expertise—such as engineers, business analysts, managers, and other stakeholders. To be effective, data professionals need strong interpersonal skills and the ability to communicate across disciplines. This includes listening carefully, understanding different viewpoints, and explaining technical ideas in plain language so that everyone can engage with the insights and contribute meaningfully. Working well in a team also means being open to feedback and flexible enough to adapt your approach based on input from others. When collaboration works well, it leads to well-rounded solutions that are both data-informed and grounded in real-world needs across the organization.

Adaptability and Continuous Learning   Data analytics is a rapidly changing field, with new tools, techniques, and technologies emerging all the time. To stay competitive and effective, data professionals need to be adaptable and committed to lifelong learning. This means keeping up with the latest developments in programming languages, statistical methods, machine learning, and data visualization. Being able to quickly pick up new skills and tools helps professionals stay relevant as the field evolves. Whether it's through online courses, conferences, or discussions with peers, continuous learning enables data experts to face new challenges, adopt the best practices, and drive innovation. Being flexible also means being comfortable switching between different projects, industries, or types of problems, always tailoring the approach to fit the situation.

Future Careers

The field of data analytics is growing rapidly, and with the increasing adoption of AI and machine learning, new career paths are emerging.

AI/ML Specialist

As artificial intelligence and machine learning continue to evolve, professionals who specialize in AI/ML technologies will be in high demand. These experts will design and develop advanced machine learning models, algorithms, and AI systems that drive intelligent automation and decision-making.

Up and Coming Data Jobs

AI/ML Specialist	• Design and develop advanced machine learning models and AI systems • Focus on intelligent automation and decision-making
Data Privacy and Ethics Officer	• Ensure compliance with data regulations (e.g., GDPR) • Safeguard ethical use of data and prevent biases in models
Data Visualization Specialist	• Create intuitive visualizations for data storytelling • Help stakeholders make data-driven decisions
Chief Data Officer (CDO)	• Oversee data strategy and governance • Manage data assets across the organization
Quantum Computing Data Analyst	• Analyze and process data from quantum systems • Leverage quantum computing for complex data analysis

Data Privacy and Ethics Officer

With the growing concerns over data privacy and security, professionals in this role will ensure that organizations comply with regulations like GDPR, and that data is used ethically and responsibly. These individuals will also ensure that machine learning models do not perpetuate bias and discrimination. GDPR (General Data Protection Regulation) is a set of data protection and privacy laws in the European Union designed to give individuals more control over their personal data and to ensure its secure handling by organizations.

Data Visualization Specialist

As the importance of data storytelling increases, there will be a growing need for professionals who specialize in data visualization. These experts will design intuitive and effective visualizations that help stakeholders quickly understand complex data and make data-driven decisions.

Chief Data Officer (CDO)

As more organizations recognize the value of data, the role of Chief Data Officer (CDO) is becoming more common. The CDO is responsible for overseeing the data strategy, governance, and management of data assets, ensuring that data is leveraged effectively across the organization.

Quantum Computing Data Analyst

Quantum computing is a type of computing that uses quantum bits (qubits) to perform calculations at speeds and complexities far beyond the capabilities of traditional computers. With the rise of quantum computing, professionals who can analyze and process data from quantum systems will become increasingly important. Quantum computing has the potential to revolutionize data analysis, and early adopters will have a significant advantage in developing this specialized skill set.

Review Questions

1. What technical skills are essential for professionals in data analytics?
2. Why is SQL an important tool for data analysts and data scientists?
3. How is machine learning used in finance and healthcare?
4. What role does data visualization play in business intelligence and decision-making?
5. What are some of the soft skills required for a successful career in data analytics?
6. What are some of the emerging career opportunities in data analytics?

1-3 Tools and Technologies

> **Learning Outcomes**
>
> **1-3-1** Identify key tools in data analytics.
> **1-3-2** Understand the role of programming languages.
> **1-3-3** Recognize data processing tools such as Hadoop, Spark, and ETL platforms.
> **1-3-4** Know popular data visualization tools.
> **1-3-5** Understand emerging tools and their potential future role.

Essential Tools

Data analytics is a constantly changing field that depends on a wide range of tools and technologies to handle, analyze, and visualize data. As the amount of data grows and the insights needed become more complex, data professionals must have the right tools to meet these challenges. These tools include programming languages, platforms for processing data, and software for creating visualizations. This section will cover the most commonly used tools in data analytics today and introduce some emerging technologies that are expected to influence the future of the industry.

Types of Tools in Data Analytics

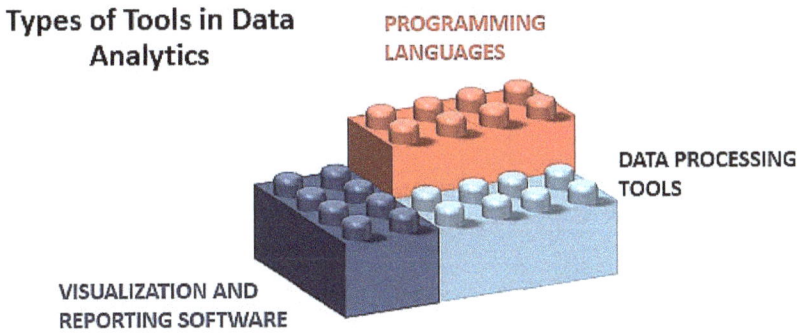

PROGRAMMING LANGUAGES

DATA PROCESSING TOOLS

VISUALIZATION AND REPORTING SOFTWARE

Programming Languages

Programming languages form the backbone of data analytics. However, in the age of AI the role of programming is likely to become highly automated. They allow professionals to manipulate, analyze, and visualize data efficiently. In the realm of data science, three programming tools stand out for their capabilities in managing data and performing complex analyses: Python, R, and SQL. Each serves a distinct purpose and plays a critical role in the workflow of data professionals.

Python has emerged as the dominant programming language for data science and machine learning due to its simplicity and versatility. Its rich ecosystem of libraries such as Pandas for data manipulation, NumPy for numerical computing, and Matplotlib and Seaborn for data visualization makes it an indispensable tool for data analysis. Furthermore, Python supports machine learning frameworks like Scikit-learn and deep learning libraries such as TensorFlow and PyTorch, positioning it as a comprehensive tool for predictive modeling and artificial intelligence development.

On the other hand, R remains a powerful tool, particularly in academia and research, where advanced statistical analyses are often required. R excels at

complex statistical modeling and is renowned for its strong visualization capabilities. Libraries like ggplot2 for creating detailed plots and dplyr for efficient data manipulation empower analysts to conduct sophisticated analyses with ease. Despite Python's popularity, R continues to be a preferred
choice for statisticians and researchers who need to apply intricate statistical techniques to their data.

Lastly, SQL (Structured Query Language) is the foundation for interacting
with relational databases. It is essential for data professionals who work
with structured data, as it allows them to query databases, perform operations like joins, filters, and aggregations, and manipulate data stored in
relational systems. SQL remains the primary language for working with traditional databases such as MySQL and PostgreSQL, as well as modern cloud-
based data warehouses like Google BigQuery and Amazon Redshift.

Data Processing Tools

Working with large datasets calls for specialized tools that can efficiently
handle and process data at scale. These tools help analysts prepare and
transform data into formats suitable for analysis, supporting organizations
in making timely, data-driven decisions.

Two popular open-source platforms for processing big data in distributed
environments are Hadoop and Spark. Hadoop offers a framework that stores
and processes data across many machines, making it easier to manage vast
datasets. Spark, however, is known for its speed, thanks to in-memory processing, which allows it to outperform Hadoop in many cases. Both platforms are essential for organizations dealing with massive amounts of data,
enabling them to perform real-time analytics and large-scale processing.

Alongside these, ETL tools like Apache Nifi and Talend play a critical role in
managing data flow. They extract data from multiple sources, convert it into
the right format for analysis, and load it into databases or data warehouses.

ETL tools are especially important for cleaning and preparing data, ensuring it's consistent and reliable. They also help integrate data from various formats and systems, which is common in complex data environments.

In summary, Hadoop, Spark, and ETL tools form the backbone for handling large datasets. They allow organizations to process, clean, and transform data efficiently, laying the groundwork for advanced analytics and quick, informed decision-making.

Example

ShopSmart, a large e-commerce company, faces the challenge of processing massive datasets for customer transactions, behavior analysis, and real-time decision-making. To solve this, they use Hadoop for scalable storage, Apache Spark for real-time data processing, and ETL tools like Apache Nifi and Talend for data integration.

Hadoop stores large volumes of data, such as transaction records and user activity, across multiple machines, while Spark processes data in real time to offer personalized recommendations and detect fraud. ETL tools like Nifi and Talend clean and integrate data from various sources, ensuring consistency and quality before analysis.

By using these technologies, ShopSmart achieves faster data processing, real-time insights, and seamless integration of data, improving inventory management, customer experiences, and fraud detection.

Visualization and Reporting Software

Once data has been processed and analyzed, communicating the findings effectively becomes essential. Data visualization tools help turn complex information into clear, engaging visuals that make it easier for stakeholders to understand and act on the insights. Some of the most widely used tools for this purpose include Tableau, Power BI, and Matplotlib/Seaborn, each offering unique features suited to different visualization needs.

Comparison of Visualization Tools

Tool	Strengths	Ideal Use Cases
Tableau	Drag-and-drop interface, dashboards	Business analytics, interactive reporting
Power BI	Microsoft integration, affordable	Small businesses, corporate reporting
Matplotlib	Customizable, scientific visualizations	Research, publication-ready charts
ggplot2	Elegant syntax, integration with R, strong themes	Academic research, statistical visualization

Tableau is widely recognized for its ability to create interactive dashboards and reports without requiring extensive programming skills. Its intuitive drag-and-drop interface makes it accessible to both data analysts and business users, facilitating the creation of dynamic visualizations. Tableau's ability to easily connect to various data sources enhances its versatility, making it an ideal tool for exploring and presenting data insights across different industries.

Similarly, Power BI, developed by Microsoft, is a powerful tool for transforming raw data into interactive reports and visualizations. Known for its business intelligence capabilities, Power BI is especially popular within organizations already using Microsoft products, such as Excel and Azure, due to its seamless integration with these tools. Its strong reporting features and cloud-based sharing capabilities make it a favored choice for businesses looking to empower their teams with data-driven insights and foster collaboration.

For data professionals who work in Python, Matplotlib and Seaborn are essential libraries for creating static, animated, and interactive visualizations. Matplotlib offers high customizability, allowing users to fine-tune their plots, while Seaborn provides a higher-level interface that simplifies the creation of more aesthetically pleasing and complex visualizations, such as heatmaps and scatter plots. Together, these libraries allow for flexible and detailed data visualizations tailored to the needs of data scientists and analysts.

> **Example**
>
> HealthPlus, a healthcare provider, uses data visualization tools like Tableau, Power BI, and Matplotlib/Seaborn to make complex patient and operational data more accessible to stakeholders, such as doctors, managers, and executives.
>
> Olivia, a data analyst, uses Tableau to create interactive dashboards that track key metrics like patient admission rates and hospital bed occupancy. These dashboards help hospital managers monitor performance in real time, allowing them to address issues like overcrowded emergency rooms or understaffed departments quickly.
>
> Carlos, the CFO, uses Power BI to create financial and operational reports, which senior management uses for budgeting and forecasting. Power BI also promotes collaboration, enabling team members to comment and align on financial data. Meanwhile, Dr. Jasmine, a data scientist, uses Matplotlib and Seaborn to create advanced visualizations, such as heatmaps and scatter plots, which help doctors understand treatment outcomes and make better decisions.
>
> By using these tools, HealthPlus improves decision-making at all levels, enhances operational efficiency, and achieves better patient outcomes through clear, actionable insights.

Up and Coming Tools

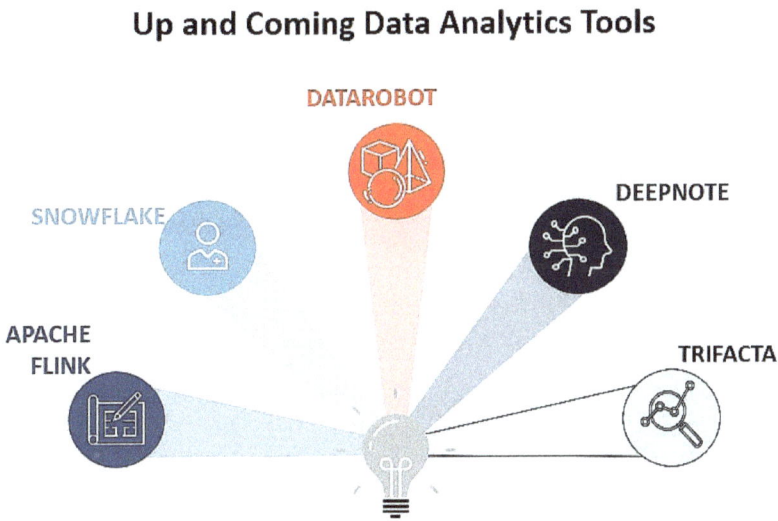

Up and Coming Data Analytics Tools

DATAROBOT

DEEPNOTE

SNOWFLAKE

APACHE
FLINK

TRIFACTA

As the field of data analytics continues to evolve, new tools are emerging to meet the growing demands of big data, real-time analytics, and artificial intelligence. Some of the up-and-coming tools that are gaining traction in the industry include:

Apache Flink

Apache Flink is an open-source stream processing platform that enables real-time analytics on data streams. Unlike batch processing, which processes data in chunks, Flink allows for real-time, low-latency data processing, making it ideal for applications in IoT, real-time fraud detection, and dynamic recommendation systems.

Snowflake

Snowflake is a cloud-based data warehousing platform that is gaining popularity due to its ability to handle large-scale data storage and processing. It enables businesses to easily scale their data infrastructure and perform analytics in the cloud with powerful features like automatic scaling and data sharing.

DataRobot

DataRobot is an automated machine learning (AutoML) platform that allows data professionals to build and deploy machine learning models without deep expertise in data science. It automates the process of model selection, training, and tuning, making it easier for organizations to apply machine learning to their data with minimal effort.

Deepnote

Deepnote is a collaborative data science notebook designed for teams. It allows users to run code, share results, and work together in real-time. It supports popular languages like Python and R and is designed to improve collaboration in data science projects.

Trifacta

Trifacta is a data wrangling tool that simplifies the process of cleaning and transforming raw data. It uses machine learning to automate data preparation tasks and offers an intuitive interface for non-technical users, making it easier for business analysts to clean and structure data for analysis.

As new tools continue to emerge the landscape of data analytics is shifting towards more advanced, automated, and real-time capabilities. Staying abreast of these tools and incorporating them into the analytics workflow will help data professionals remain competitive and drive meaningful insights in the AI-powered future.

Example

BrightMart, a growing e-commerce platform, is leveraging emerging data analytics tools to optimize its operations, enhance decision-making, and stay competitive in the market. David, a data engineer, integrates Apache Flink for real-time data processing, enabling the company to monitor customer interactions, detect fraud instantly, and personalize product recommendations based on live data. This not only reduces fraud by 40customer demand in real-time.

Maria, a data analyst, migrates the company's data to Snowflake, a cloud-based data warehousing platform, allowing the company to scale its data infrastructure as needed. This transition enables BrightMart to handle large datasets efficiently, especially during peak events like Black Friday, and share data securely with external partners for collaboration. Meanwhile, James, a data scientist, adopts DataRobot's AutoML capabilities to speed up model development, reducing the time spent on creating predictive models for customer lifetime value and churn prediction by 50decision-making.

Rachel, another data scientist, uses Deepnote to facilitate collaboration among team members by running complex scripts and sharing interactive visualizations. This real-time collaboration accelerates the decision-making process and ensures alignment across departments. Additionally, Alan, a business analyst, utilizes Trifacta to automate data wrangling tasks, significantly speeding up the data preparation process by 60analysis. These combined tools allow BrightMart to streamline operations, improve customer experiences through personalized recommendations, and enhance overall business performance.

Review Questions

1. What are the main programming languages used in data analytics?
2. How do Hadoop and Spark aid in data processing?
3. What role do ETL tools play in data workflows?
4. How are Matplotlib and Seaborn used in Python for visualization?
5. What is Apache Flink used for?
6. What is Snowflake's role in data processing?
7. How does DataRobot simplify machine learning?
8. What does Trifacta do for data preparation?

Chapter 2

Understanding Data

Understanding data is foundational for data analysis, machine learning, and any form of advanced data processing. The structure, type, and organization of data significantly impact how it can be processed, analyzed, and leveraged for decision-making. This section delves into the different types of data, the distinction between structured and unstructured data, and how structured data is manipulated.

2-1 Types of Data

Learning Outcomes
2-1-1 Understand the differences between quantitative and qualitative data.
2-1-2 Recognize the subtypes of quantitative data (discrete and continuous).
2-1-3 Identify the subtypes of qualitative data (nominal and ordinal).
2-1-4 Explain what unstructured data is.

The primary categories of data include quantitative and qualitative data, as well as categorical and continuous data. Each type of data serves different analytical purposes and requires different processing techniques.

Quantitative vs. Qualitative Data

Quantitative Data

Quantitative data is numeric and measurable. This type of data represents quantities and is used in mathematical calculations. Quantitative data can be classified into two main subtypes:

Discrete Data   This subset of quantitative data consists of countable values. Discrete data includes whole numbers or counts, such as the number of students in a class or the number of products sold. It cannot take fractional or decimal values.

Quantitative vs Qualitative Data Examples

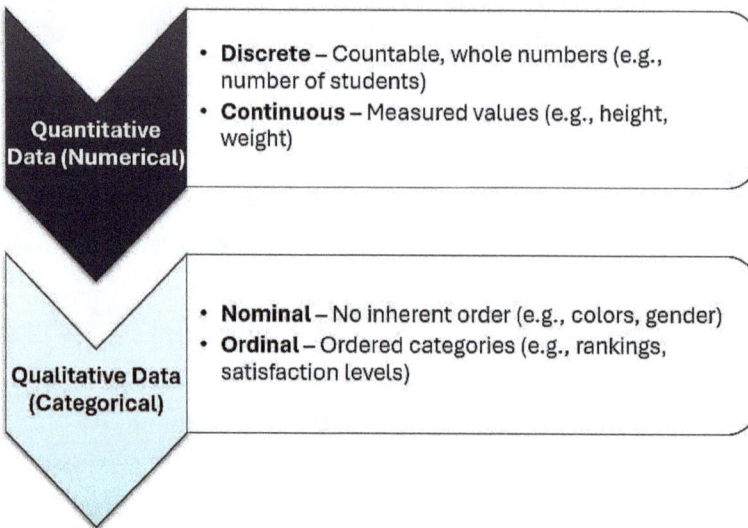

Quantitative Data (Numerical)
- **Discrete** – Countable, whole numbers (e.g., number of students)
- **Continuous** – Measured values (e.g., height, weight)

Qualitative Data (Categorical)
- **Nominal** – No inherent order (e.g., colors, gender)
- **Ordinal** – Ordered categories (e.g., rankings, satisfaction levels)

Continuous Data   Continuous data is measurable and can take any value within a given range. This type of data is more precise and includes variables like weight, height, time, or temperature, where measurements can have decimal values and represent a continuous spectrum.

Example

Sarah a café owner, analyzes sales data to improve business operations.

Discrete Data Example:

Sarah tracks the number of customers visiting her café each day. On Monday, she records 85 customers, and on Tuesday, 92 customers. Since customers are counted as whole numbers, this is discrete data.

Continuous Data Example:

Sarah also monitors the amount of coffee poured into each cup. A small cup might contain 8.5 ounces, while a large cup holds 12.3 ounces. Since coffee volume can be measured in decimals and exists on a continuous scale, this is continuous data.

Qualitative Data

Qualitative data, also known as categorical data, represents qualities or characteristics rather than quantities. This data cannot be directly measured or counted. It is often used to describe attributes or features. Qualitative data can be further classified into two types:

Nominal Data   Nominal data consists of categories that have no inherent order or ranking. Examples of nominal data include gender, nationality, or colors. The categories are simply labels without any relative importance or sequence.

Ordinal Data   Ordinal data refers to categories that have a natural order or ranking. However, the intervals between the categories are not necessarily consistent. Examples include rating scales (e.g., "low," "medium," "high") or education levels (e.g., "high school," "bachelor's degree," "master's degree").

Example

Doug, a restaurant manager, collects customer feedback to improve service.

Doug surveys customers about their preferred cuisine type at the restaurant. The responses include Italian, Mexican, Chinese, and Indian. Since these are categories without any inherent ranking, this is nominal data.

Doug also asks customers to rate their dining experience using a scale: "Poor," "Fair," "Good," "Very Good," and "Excellent." These ratings have a natural order (from worst to best), but the difference between "Good" and "Very Good" may not be the same as between "Fair" and "Good." This makes it ordinal data

---

Unstructured data

Unstructured data is typically qualitative in nature. It includes information that doesn't have a predefined structure, such as text, images, audio, or video, which often require interpretation to extract meaningful insights. For example, text data from social media posts, customer reviews, or speech recordings are qualitative because they involve subjective content, opinions, and descriptions that don't fit neatly into rows and columns.

However, unstructured data can sometimes contain quantitative aspects, like numbers or statistics embedded within text, but its primary form is qualitative. When processing unstructured data, techniques like natural language processing (NLP) or image recognition are often used to analyze and extract useful patterns or structures from this qualitative content.

Example

Emma Reynolds, a marketing manager for a retail brand, wants to under-stand customer opinions about her company's latest product launch.

She collects thousands of social media comments, tweets, and customer reviews from platforms like Twitter, Facebook, and Instagram. These con-tain a mix of text, emojis, images, and even video testimonials. This is all unstructured data.

Review Questions

1. What is quantitative data, and what are its two main subtypes?
2. What is the difference between discrete and continuous data?
3. What is qualitative data, and how is it different from quantitative data?
4. What are the two types of qualitative data?
5. How is unstructured data related to qualitative data?

2-2 Structured vs. Unstructured Data

Learning Outcomes

2-2-1 Understand the differences between structured and unstructured data.

2-2-2 Identify examples of structured and unstructured data.

2-2-3 Recognize how structured data is stored and processed.

2-2-4 Learn how unstructured data is processed using advanced techniques.

Data can be classified based on its organization and format, which significantly influences how it is processed and analyzed. The two primary categories of data are structured and unstructured data. Each type has its characteristics and requires different techniques for efficient processing and analysis.

Comparing Structured and Unstructured Data

Category	Structured Data	Unstructured Data
Format	Organized, tabular	Free-form, no fixed structure
Examples	Spreadsheets, SQL DBs	Emails, images, videos
Storage	Relational databases	Data lakes, NoSQL, cloud storage
Processing	Easy analysis (SQL)	Requires AI, NLP, data mining

Structured Data

Definition

Structured data refers to data that is organized in a predefined format, typically arranged in rows and columns. This format is often used in relational databases, spreadsheets, and CSV files. Structured data follows a specific schema, meaning that each data element fits into a predefined structure with clearly defined data types (e.g., integers, strings, dates). This organization makes structured data easy to process and manipulate using standard tools and programming languages, such as SQL.

Common examples of structured data include customer information stored in CRM systems (such as name, age, address), financial data, sales transactions, and inventory records. These datasets are highly organized and straightforward to work with.

Databases and Data Warehouses

Structured data is typically stored in relational databases such as MySQL or PostgreSQL, or in data warehouses like Amazon Redshift or Google BigQuery. These systems use SQL (Structured Query Language) to access, retrieve, and manipulate data efficiently. Relational databases offer easy access and quick retrieval of data, which is vital for businesses and organizations to make data-driven decisions.

Handling Structured Data

Structured Data Processing Steps

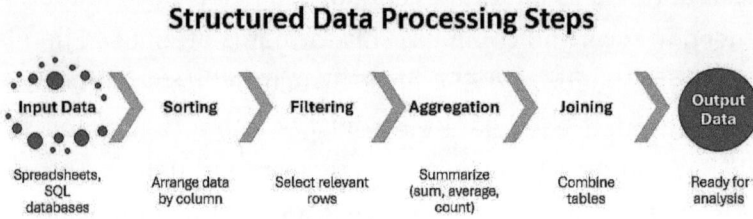

Input Data	Sorting	Filtering	Aggregation	Joining	Output Data
Spreadsheets, SQL databases	Arrange data by column	Select relevant rows	Summarize (sum, average, count)	Combine tables	Ready for analysis

Structured data is processed through common operations such as sorting, filtering, joining, and aggregation. These operations are simple due to the data's well-defined structure, which makes it easier to extract insights and perform complex queries.

Example

Structured Data for a Retail Business

Structured data can be stored in relational databases like MySQL or PostgreSQL for easy management and retrieval. The data is stored in tables, where each table represents an entity, such as Customers or Sales Transactions. For example, the Customers table can be linked to the Sales Transactions table by the Customer ID, allowing quick access to transaction details for a specific customer.

Customer Information:

Customer ID	First Name	Last Name	Age	Address	Phone Number	Email Address
101	John	Doe	35	123 Elm St, NY	555-1234	john.doe@email.com
102	Jane	Smith	29	456 Oak St, NY	555-5678	jane.smith@email.com
103	Michael	Johnson	45	789 Pine St, LA	555-9101	michael.j@email.com

Sales Transactions:

Order ID	Customer ID	Product	Quantity	Total Price	Date
001	101	Laptop	1	$1,200	2025-03-01
002	102	T-shirt	2	$40	2025-03-02
003	103	Phone	1	$800	2025-03-03
004	101	Headphones	1	$150	2025-03-04

Unstructured Data

Definition

Unstructured data doesn't follow a fixed format or organization like structured data does. It comes in many different forms—such as text, images, audio, and video—which makes it more complex to handle. Because it doesn't fit neatly into rows and columns, traditional methods for storing and analyzing data often fall short. To make sense of unstructured data, specialized tools and techniques are needed. Examples include text documents, emails, social media posts, photos, videos, and audio recordings. These types of data require advanced processing to uncover meaningful insights.

Handling Unstructured Data

Text Data: Analyzing and extracting information from text data requires techniques like Natural Language Processing (NLP). NLP can be used for tasks such as sentiment analysis, topic modeling, and text classification, helping organizations understand customer feedback, market trends, or detect patterns in written content.

Image Data: Computer vision techniques are used to process and analyze image data. These methods often employ convolutional neural networks (CNNs) to recognize patterns, classify objects, or detect anomalies in images. For example, image recognition can be used in medical diagnostics to identify conditions from medical imaging.

Processing Image Data

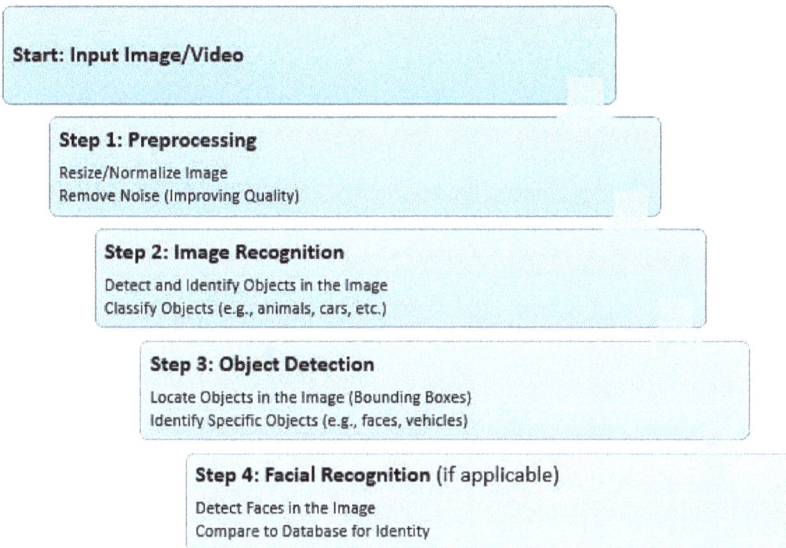

Start: Input Image/Video

Step 1: Preprocessing

Resize/Normalize Image
Remove Noise (Improving Quality)

Step 2: Image Recognition

Detect and Identify Objects in the Image
Classify Objects (e.g., animals, cars, etc.)

Step 3: Object Detection

Locate Objects in the Image (Bounding Boxes)
Identify Specific Objects (e.g., faces, vehicles)

Step 4: Facial Recognition (if applicable)

Detect Faces in the Image
Compare to Database for Identity

Audio and Video Data: Unstructured audio data is typically processed through speech recognition systems, enabling applications like voice assistants (e.g., Siri or Alexa). Video data is analyzed using techniques such as object detection or action recognition, which are important for applications like surveillance, autonomous vehicles, and content summarization.

Example

Types of Unstructured Data

Text Data (e.g., Social Media Posts):

Tweets, Facebook posts, or blog articles are examples of unstructured text data. They don't fit into rows or columns and can be analyzed using tools like Natural Language Processing (NLP).

Image Data (e.g., Instagram Photos):

Pictures shared on social media platforms like Instagram are unstructured. Computer Vision tools can be used to analyze images and identify objects or scenes.

Audio Data (e.g., Voice Messages):

Voice messages sent through apps like WhatsApp are unstructured. Speech recognition technology can convert speech into text.

Video Data (e.g., YouTube Videos):

Videos uploaded to YouTube or other platforms are unstructured data. Video analysis tools can detect objects or actions within the video.

Review Questions

1. What is structured data, and how is it organized?
2. Can you give examples of structured data?
3. Where is structured data typically stored?
4. What are common operations performed on structured data?
5. What is unstructured data, and how does it differ from structured data?
6. Can you give examples of unstructured data?

2-3 Structured Data Manipulation

> **Learning Outcomes**
>
> **2-3-1** Understand how structured data is organized in rows and columns.
> **2-3-2** Recognize why indexing and organizing data is important.
> **2-3-3** Perform basic data tasks like sorting, filtering, grouping, and join-ing.

This section explores how structured data is represented and how it can be manipulated to make it suitable for analysis and machine learning tasks.

Tabular Data Representation

Rows and Columns

In structured data, the most common way to represent information is in the form of rows and columns. Each row represents a single record or instance, while each column represents a specific attribute or feature associated with the records. For example, consider a dataset of employees in a company. Each row would represent an individual employee, and the columns might represent various attributes such as employee ID, name, department, and salary. This tabular format helps in organizing data systematically, where each record is represented by a unique set of attributes.

Tabular Representation

Structured data is typically organized in tables because this format is straightforward and compatible with most database systems and analysis tools. Tables make it easier to store, retrieve, and work with data efficiently. Whether using relational databases or programming libraries like pandas in Python or dplyr in R, the tabular layout supports common operations such as sorting, filtering, and aggregating data. This flexibility makes it a go-to format for many data analysis tasks.

Data Indexing and Organization

Indexing

Indexing is a technique used to optimize the retrieval of data from large datasets. An index is a data structure that allows for fast searching and retrieval based on the values of one or more columns in the table. For instance, in a database with thousands of employee records, creating an index on the "employee ID" column allows for quick lookups of a specific employee's information without needing to scan every record. Indexing can significantly improve the performance of queries, especially in large datasets, making it an essential tool for efficient data management.

Example

Index on Employee ID:

Employee ID	First Name	Last Name	Department	Salary
1001	John	Doe	Sales	$60,000
1002	Jane	Smith	HR	$55,000
1003	Mike	Johnson	IT	$70,000
1004	Sarah	Williams	Marketing	$65,000
1005	Tom	Brown	Sales	$58,000

Having an index on the Employee ID allows the system to quickly find records by searching directly for an ID without needing to scan every record in the table.

Example query: Find Employee with ID = 1003

The index immediately points to Mike Johnson, reducing retrieval time

Data Organization

Organizing structured data properly is essential for keeping it efficient and reliable. When data is well arranged, tasks like retrieving, sorting, and filtering become faster and easier—important steps in any analysis. A clean, organized dataset is simple to navigate, helps avoid duplication, and reduces the chance of errors or inconsistencies. This includes using consistent naming, assigning correct data types to each column, and grouping related information together. Good data organization also plays a crucial role in ensuring that analyses and machine learning models based on the data are accurate, since poorly organized data can lead to misleading or incorrect conclusions.

Example

Without a grouping variable this data is hard to do aggregate analysis on products

Order ID	Product Name	Region	Sale Date	Sale Amount
001	Laptop	North America	2025-03-01	$1,200
002	T-shirt	Europe	2025-03-02	$50
003	Phone	North America	2025-03-01	$800
004	Shoes	Asia	2025-03-05	$120
005	Monitor	Europe	2025-03-04	$300

Adding product category organizes the product data

Order ID	Product Category	Product Name	Region	Sale Date	Sale Amount
001	Electronics	Laptop	North America	2025-03-01	$1,200
003	Electronics	Phone	North America	2025-03-01	$800
004	Apparel	Shoes	Asia	2025-03-05	$120
002	Apparel	T-shirt	Europe	2025-03-02	$50
005	Electronics	Monitor	Europe	2025-03-04	$300

Basic Data Operations

Once data is organized and indexed, various basic operations can be performed to manipulate and prepare the data for analysis. These operations include sorting, filtering, aggregation, and joining, all of which help in deriving useful insights from the data.

Sorting

Sorting is the process of arranging data in a specific order, either ascending or descending, based on one or more columns. Sorting is useful for organizing data in a way that makes analysis easier. For example, sorting sales data by date helps to analyze trends over time, while sorting data by product can help identify which products are performing the best. Sorting operations are commonly used to ensure that data is presented in a logical order, making it easier to identify patterns or outliers.

Example

Sorting data by sales makes it easy to identify top sales

Order ID	Customer Name	Region	Total Sales	Product Category	Date
005	Tom Brown	North America	$2,000	Electronics	2025-03-05
003	Michael Lee	North America	$1,800	Furniture	2025-03-03
001	John Doe	North America	$1,200	Electronics	2025-03-01
004	Sarah Kim	Asia	$750	Electronics	2025-03-04
002	Jane Smith	Europe	$500	Apparel	2025-03-02

Filtering

Filtering allows analysts to extract only the relevant subset of data from a larger dataset. This operation helps in narrowing down data to focus on specific criteria. For instance, filtering sales data to include only records from a particular region or customers who made purchases above a certain threshold enables a more focused analysis. By filtering out irrelevant data, analysts can concentrate on what matters, leading to more targeted and insightful results.

Example

Unfiltered data

Order ID	Customer Name	Region	Total Sales	Product Category	Date
001	John Doe	North America	$1,200	Electronics	2025-03-01
002	Jane Smith	Europe	$500	Apparel	2025-03-02
003	Michael Lee	North America	$1,800	Furniture	2025-03-03
004	Sarah Kim	Asia	$750	Electronics	2025-03-04
005	Tom Brown	North America	$2,000	Electronics	2025-03-05

Filtered by region helps to focus on specific data

Order ID	Customer Name	Region	Total Sales	Product Category	Date
001	John Doe	North America	$1,200	Electronics	2025-03-01
003	Michael Lee	North America	$1,800	Furniture	2025-03-03
005	Tom Brown	North America	$2,000	Electronics	2025-03-05

Aggregation

Aggregation means summarizing data to calculate important measures like averages, totals, or counts. It helps reveal patterns and trends in large datasets. For instance, grouping sales data by region can show how much each area contributes to overall sales, giving businesses a clearer picture of regional performance. Other examples include finding the average salary within each department or counting how many transactions each customer has made. Aggregation is a key step in making large datasets easier to understand and is often used before diving into deeper analysis. Below is an example demonstrating how sales data can be summarized by region and average salaries calculated by department.

Example

Data aggregated by region on total sales for that region

Region	Total Sales	Number of Transactions
North America	$500,000	150
Europe	$350,000	120
Asia	$450,000	130
South America	$300,000	100
Australia	$250,000	80

Joining

Joining refers to the process of merging data from different tables using a shared attribute. For example, a company might have one table with customer details and another with sales records. By joining these tables on a common column like customer ID, analysts can connect customer information with their sales history. Joins are essential for combining data from multiple sources and are a fundamental part of working with relational databases and performing data analysis.

Example

If a company has a separate Customer table and a Sales table, a join can be used to combine these tables based on a common column, such as Customer ID.

Customer table

Customer ID	Name	Email
1	John Doe	john.doe@email.com
2	Jane Smith	jane.smith@email.com
3	Bob Brown	bob.brown@email.com

Sales table

Sale ID	Customer ID	Product	Amount
101	1	Laptop	1000
102	2	Smartphone	600
103	1	Tablet	300

Joined table

Customer ID	Name	Email	Sale ID	Product	Amount
1	John Doe	john.doe@email.com	101	Laptop	1000
1	John Doe	john.doe@email.com	103	Tablet	300
2	Jane Smith	jane.smith@email.com	102	Smartphone	600

This allows analysts to examine the relationship between customer information and their corresponding sales activity.

Review Questions

1. What do rows and columns represent in structured data?
2. Why is the tabular format used for structured data?
3. What is indexing, and how does it make data easier to find?
4. How does organizing data help with analysis?
5. What is sorting, and why is it useful for data analysis?
6. How does filtering help you focus on important data?
7. What is aggregation, and how is it used to summarize data?

2-4 Using Unstructured Data

Learning Outcomes

2-4-1 Understand the challenges of processing unstructured data in AI.
2-4-2 Recognize the key applications of unstructured data.
2-4-3 Identify AI techniques used to process unstructured data.
2-4-4 Understand how deep learning models are used in processing unstructured data.

Unstructured data includes text, images, audio, and video, and its unorganized nature makes it more complex to process. However, despite the challenges it poses, unstructured data holds immense value for various AI applications, making it a critical area of focus for AI development.

Challenges with Unstructured Data

Unstructured data presents unique challenges because it doesn't have the clear organization that structured data offers. Often messy and high-dimensional, it can't be easily processed using traditional methods. To work with unstructured data, AI models first need to preprocess it, turning it into a format that's easier to analyze. This step can be resource-intensive and requires advanced algorithms, especially when dealing with large volumes of data. For example, when handling text, AI systems must identify key elements like keywords, entities, and sentiment from the raw input. Similarly, images and videos need to be analyzed to recognize objects, scenes, and patterns before any specific tasks can be performed. These processes rely on sophisticated models that can efficiently handle large amounts of unstructured data.

Applications of Unstructured Data

Despite its complexity, unstructured data can provide valuable insights when processed correctly. AI has made significant strides in analyzing unstructured data across various domains. Some of the key applications include:

Text Data: Natural Language Processing (NLP)

Natural Language Processing (NLP) allows AI systems to process and under-stand human language. Text data is abundant, with applications such as customer reviews, social media posts, and documents offering rich sources of information. NLP techniques enable AI to perform tasks like sentiment analysis, text classification, and machine translation. For example, senti-ment analysis allows businesses to gauge public opinion about their prod-ucts, while machine translation enables real-time communication between people who speak different languages. NLP is the backbone of many AI-powered chatbots, virtual assistants, and language translation tools.

> **Example**
>
> Sentiment Analysis for Product Reviews
>
> Amazon uses NLP to analyze millions of customer reviews to determine sentiment trends. By categorizing reviews as positive, negative, or neutral, Amazon gains insights into customer satisfaction, common complaints, and potential product improvements. This analysis helps businesses make data-driven decisions about product features, pricing, and marketing strategies.

Image Data: Computer Vision

Computer Vision is an AI field that focuses on enabling machines to interpret and understand visual information. With image data, AI can perform tasks like object detection, facial recognition, and image classification. These applications are widely used in industries ranging from healthcare to security. For instance, in healthcare, AI can analyze medical images like X-rays and MRIs to detect anomalies or diseases. In security, AI can use facial recognition to identify individuals in surveillance footage. The ability to analyze and interpret images allows AI to make decisions based on visual data, enhancing automation and improving efficiency.

Example

AI-Powered Cancer Detection

Hospitals use AI-driven computer vision to analyze MRI scans, mammograms, and X-rays for early disease detection. For instance, Google's DeepMind developed an AI model that detects breast cancer in mammograms more accurately than radiologists. This reduces false positives and negatives, leading to faster diagnoses and better patient outcomes.

Audio Data: Speech Recognition

Speech recognition is another significant application of AI that processes unstructured audio data. AI systems are designed to understand spoken language and convert it into text. This technology is widely used in voice assistants like Siri, Alexa, and Google Assistant, where users can speak commands and have the AI respond accordingly. Additionally, speech recognition is used for transcription services, converting spoken words into written text. This application is particularly useful for improving accessibility and automating tasks like note-taking, customer service interactions, and content generation.

Example

AI-Powered Customer Service at Banks

Banks like JPMorgan Chase use speech recognition AI to transcribe and analyze customer calls in real-time. AI can detect keywords related to fraud, dissatisfaction, or service issues, helping customer service teams quickly address concerns and improve service quality. Additionally, speech analytics can identify common pain points and trends to optimize support strategies.

Video Data: Video Analysis

Video data is often used in surveillance, sports analysis, and autonomous vehicles. AI can analyze video footage to detect actions, track objects, or summarize video content. In surveillance, AI can automatically detect suspicious activities in real-time, reducing the need for human intervention. In sports, AI can analyze player movements and provide insights on performance. Autonomous vehicles also rely heavily on AI to interpret video data from cameras and sensors to make decisions about navigation and safety.

Example

Tesla's Self-Driving Car System

Tesla's Autopilot and Full Self-Driving (FSD) system uses AI to process video feeds from multiple cameras. The AI analyzes road signs, lane markings, traffic patterns, and pedestrian movements to make real-time driving decisions. This reduces accidents, enhances safety, and paves the way for fully autonomous vehicles.

AI Techniques for Processing Unstructured Data

To process unstructured data, AI employs several advanced techniques, often leveraging deep learning models. Some of the most commonly used methods include:

Convolutional Neural Networks (CNNs)

CNNs are primarily used for image and video data analysis. These deep learning models are designed to recognize patterns in visual data by using convolutional layers to detect features such as edges, textures, and shapes. CNNs have revolutionized the field of computer vision, enabling tasks like object detection, image segmentation, and facial recognition with high accuracy.

> **Example**
>
> Diagnosing diseases from medical scans
>
> CNNs are widely used in radiology to analyze X-rays, MRIs, and CT scans. AI models like Google's DeepMind have developed CNN-based systems that can detect retinal diseases, lung cancer, and brain tumors with high accuracy. For instance, CNNs power AI-assisted diagnostic tools that help doctors detect pneumonia from chest X-rays faster and with greater accuracy than traditional methods.

Recurrent Neural Networks (RNNs)

RNNs are used for sequential data, such as text and speech. Unlike traditional neural networks, RNNs can process data sequences, making them ideal for applications in Natural Language Processing (NLP) and speech recognition. They are particularly useful for tasks that require an understanding of context, such as sentiment analysis or machine translation, where the meaning of a word can depend on the words that came before or after it.

> **Example**
>
> Virtual Assistants like Siri, Alexa, and Google Assistant
>
> RNNs, particularly Long Short-Term Memory (LSTM) networks, enable speech-to-text conversion in virtual assistants. These models allow devices to understand spoken language, process commands, and respond appropriately. Google's speech recognition system, used in Google Assistant, relies on RNN-based models to improve real-time transcription accuracy.

Transformer Models

Transformer models have transformed natural language processing (NLP) and are now widely applied across many tasks involving unstructured data, such as language translation, text summarization, sentiment analysis, and even image and multimodal processing. Unlike earlier models like RNNs and LSTMs, Transformers use attention mechanisms—especially self-attention—to evaluate how different parts of the input relate to each other. This approach helps them better understand long-range connections and the context within data.

One key advantage of Transformers is their ability to process entire sequences simultaneously instead of one step at a time. This makes training and prediction faster and allows them to handle very large, complex datasets, such as vast collections of documents, social media feeds, or multilingual text. Transformer architectures are also flexible enough to be adapted for various data types, including text, images, audio, and even structured formats like tables or graphs when represented properly.

Models based on Transformers, like OpenAI's GPT and Google's BERT, have set new benchmarks in NLP performance. They benefit from large-scale pre-training on unstructured data and can be fine-tuned for specific tasks using relatively small amounts of additional data. This makes them especially useful for organizations dealing with messy, unlabeled, or mixed-format datasets.

Example

Chatbots and AI-powered customer service

Transformer-based models like GPT (used in OpenAI's ChatGPT) and BERT (used in Google Search) have transformed customer support. Many companies, such as Bank of America (Erica) and IBM Watson, deploy AI chatbots that understand and respond to customer inquiries using transformer models. These bots can process, understand, and generate human-like responses, reducing wait times and improving customer experience. text processing.

Review Questions

1. Name at least two applications of AI in processing text data.
2. How is AI used in analyzing image data?
3. What are some key uses of AI in processing audio data?
4. List uses of RNN/CNN models in AI.
5. What makes Transformer models more efficient?

Chapter 3

Statistical Concepts

3-1 Descriptive Statistics

Descriptive statistics are used to summarize and provide a clear understanding of the key features of a dataset. They help to interpret large amounts of data by identifying central trends, variability, and other patterns that can inform decision-making and model-building processes.

Measures of Central Tendency

Measures of central tendency are statistics that describe the "center" or average of a dataset. Measures of central tendency are statistics that describe the "center" or average of a dataset. They help us understand what a typical or common value looks like in a group of numbers.

Understanding central tendency helps in decision-making, especially in business, education, healthcare, and many other fields. It helps quickly understand what is normal or expected in a dataset.

Measures of Central Tendency

Mean

The mean is the arithmetic average of a dataset, calculated by summing all values and dividing by the number of data points. It is particularly useful for continuous data and gives a general idea of the data's central location. However, the mean can be heavily influenced by outliers or extreme values, which is why it may not always represent the true center of the data, especially in skewed distributions.

Median

The median is the middle value of a sorted dataset, dividing the data into two equal halves. If the dataset contains an even number of values, the median is the average of the two central values. The median is particularly useful when dealing with skewed distributions or data with outliers, as it is less sensitive to extreme values compared to the mean. This makes it a more robust measure of central tendency for non-normally distributed data.

Mode

The mode refers to the value that appears most frequently in a dataset. Unlike the mean and median, the mode is useful for categorical data where numerical averages do not apply. It can be helpful for identifying the most common category or value in the data, such as the most popular product purchased by customers or the most common type of customer complaint.

Measures of Dispersion

While measures of central tendency describe the center of the data, measures of dispersion help understand how spread out the data is. These measures provide insights into the variability or diversity within the dataset, which is essential for assessing how representative the mean or median might be for the entire dataset.

Standard Deviation

$$s = \sqrt{\frac{\sum (x - \bar{x})^2}{n - 1}}$$

The standard deviation measures the average distance of each data point from the mean. It is a crucial statistic for understanding the spread of data and the degree of variation within a dataset. A high standard deviation indicates that the data points are spread out from the mean, while a low standard deviation suggests that the data points are clustered closely around the mean.

Variance

Variance is the square of the standard deviation and provides an overall measure of how data points differ from the mean. While the standard deviation is often more intuitive to interpret, variance can still be valuable in understanding the data s variability. Both variance and standard deviation are crucial for assessing the stability and predictability of data before applying machine learning models.

Example

A tech company develops a recommendation system to suggest products to users based on their browsing history. To evaluate how well the system is performing, they analyze user engagement data, focusing on metrics like the average time spent on product pages, the number of items clicked, and the frequency of purchases.

Mean The average number of items clicked per user is calculated as the mean. After collecting data from 10,000 users, the mean number of items clicked is found to be 3.2. This means that on average, each user clicks 3.2 items in the recommendation system.

Median To avoid skewed results due to a few users who click many items, the median is calculated. The median number of items clicked is 2, meaning that half the users click fewer than 2 items and half click more. This is useful because it is less affected by extreme click behavior.

Mode The mode helps identify the most common user behavior. In this case, the mode of the number of items clicked is 1, as the majority of users tend to click only one product per session.

Standard Deviation The standard deviation of clicks per user is calculated to measure the spread of engagement. If the standard deviation is high, it indicates that user engagement is quite varied (some users click many products while others click very few). A low standard deviation would suggest that most users engage similarly with the system.

Review Questions

1. What are the three ways to find the center of a dataset?
2. When is the median better than the mean?
3. What does standard deviation tell you about data?
4. How are variance and standard deviation different?

3-2 Probability and Distributions

Learning Outcomes

3-2-1 Know how probability and distributions are used in machine learning.

3-2-2 Apply Bayes' theorem in machine learning.

Probability theory plays a pivotal role in machine learning, as it helps estimate the likelihood of various outcomes. In machine learning, probabilities
are used to make predictions, estimate the chances of different events, and
evaluate model performance. Several probability distributions are foundational for machine learning algorithms.

Normal Distribution

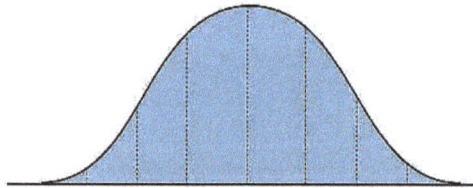

The normal distribution, often called the Gaussian distribution, is one of
the most important probability distributions in statistics. It has a symmet-
ric, bell-shaped curve where most values cluster near the mean, and fewer
values appear as you move further from the center. Many machine learning
methods, like linear regression, rely on the assumption that data follows a
normal distribution because it simplifies calculations and improves modeling efficiency.

Knowing whether data fits a normal distribution is important for a variety of statistical tests and machine learning models. For example, in linear regression, assuming normality helps ensure that the estimates of parameters and the results of hypothesis tests are reliable.

Bernoulli Distribution

The Bernoulli distribution is used to model binary outcomes or events that can only take two possible outcomes, such as "success" or "failure," "yes" or "no," or "1" and "0." In machine learning, this distribution is foundational for binary classification tasks, such as predicting whether a customer will purchase a product or not. The Bernoulli distribution forms the basis of algorithms like logistic regression, where the goal is to model the probability of one of the two possible outcomes based on input features.

Example

Scenario: A model is used to classify credit card transactions as either fraudulent or non-fraudulent (fraud = 1, non-fraud = 0).

Bernoulli Distribution Use: In fraud detection, the model assumes that each transaction either falls into the "fraudulent" class (success) or "non-fraudulent" class (failure). The model calculates the probability of a transaction being fraudulent (success) based on features like transaction amount, merchant type, and location. This is modeled using the Bernoulli distribution.

Why It Matters: The Bernoulli distribution is used because each transaction is binary—fraud or no fraud—and this allows the model to output a probability for the likelihood of fraud. Using this probability, the model can make decisions on whether to flag a transaction as fraudulent.

Bayes Theorem

Bayes' theorem is a key idea in probability and machine learning that helps calculate the likelihood of a hypothesis based on prior knowledge and new evidence. Simply put, it offers a way to update what we believe about a situation as fresh data comes in.

In machine learning, Bayes' theorem is the foundation of probabilistic models like Naive Bayes and Bayesian Networks. These models use the theorem to revise their predictions by adjusting prior assumptions according to the data they observe. For instance, a spam email filter can improve its accuracy by continuously updating its judgment on whether a message is spam as it processes more emails.

Bayesian methods are particularly useful when dealing with uncertainty or incomplete information, providing a clear framework to incorporate new data into decision-making. This adaptability makes them well-suited for practical uses such as recommendation systems, fraud detection, and predictive analytics.

> **Example**
>
> Imagine you want to predict if an email is spam based on the word "free" appearing in it.
>
> Bayes' Theorem Formula:
>
> $$P(H|E) = \frac{P(E|H) \cdot P(H)}{P(E)}$$
>
> Where:

- P(H|E) is the probability the email is spam (H) given it contains the word "free" (E).

- P(E|H) is the probability that the word "free" appears in spam.

- P(H) is the prior probability that any email is spam.

- P(E) is the probability that the word "free" appears in any email.

Given Information:

- P(H) = 0.10 (10 percent of emails are spam)

- P(E|H) = 0.70 (70 percent of spam emails contain "free")

- P(E|¬H) = 0.05 (5 percent of non-spam emails contain "free")

- P(E) = 0.30 (30 percent of all emails contain "free")

Apply Bayes' Theorem:

$$P(H|E) = \frac{0.70 \cdot 0.10}{0.30} = 0.2333$$

Interpretation:

The probability that an email is spam, given it contains the word "free," is about 23.3 percent. This shows that, despite the word "free" being common in spam, the overall low likelihood of spam emails means the word alone isn't enough to classify it as spam.

3-3 Correlation and Causality

Learning Outcomes

3-3-1 Understand the difference between correlation and causality.

3-3-2 Use correlation coefficients to analyze relationships between variables.

3-3-3 Identify the importance of correlation for feature selection.

3-3-4 Understand how causal inference improves decision-making in AI.

Correlation and Causation

Two variables move together, but no direct cause.

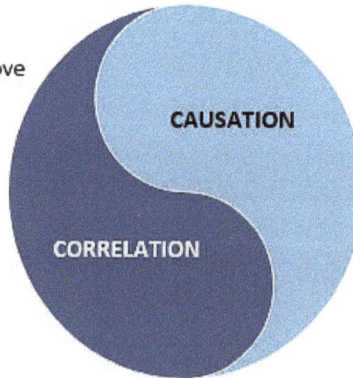

CAUSATION

One variable directly affects the other.

CORRELATION

Correlation

Correlation is a statistical concept that shows how strongly two variables are related and whether they move together in the same or opposite directions. In AI and machine learning, understanding correlation is important for choosing the right features, improving model accuracy, and spotting connections within data. By examining correlation, you can gain insights into how one variable might influence or be linked to another, helping to better understand the data's underlying patterns.

Correlation Coefficients

A correlation coefficient is a numerical value that quantifies the degree to which two variables are related. There are various types of correlation coefficients, but the most used are Pearson's correlation coefficient and Spearman s rank correlation coefficient.

Pearson's Correlation Coefficient   Pearson s correlation is the most widely known and used measure of correlation. It calculates the strength and direction of the linear relationship between two continuous variables. The value of Pearson s correlation coefficient ranges from -1 to +1. A value of +1 indicates a perfect positive linear relationship, -1 represents a perfect negative linear relationship, and 0 suggests no linear relationship between the variables. Pearson s correlation assumes that the relationship between the variables is linear and that the variables are normally distributed.

Spearman's Rank Correlation Coefficient   Spearman s rank correlation, on the other hand, is used when the relationship between the variables is not necessarily linear, or when the variables are ordinal rather than continuous. Spearman s coefficient calculates the relationship based on the ranked values of the data, making it a non-parametric measure of correlation. It is particularly useful when dealing with skewed distributions or non-normal data.

Correlation in Machine Learning and Feature Selection

In AI and machine learning, understanding correlation is key for feature selection, which is the process of choosing the most relevant features (variables) for training a model. Highly correlated features can often provide
redundant information, which may not improve the performance of a model
and can even lead to overfitting. For example, if two features in a dataset
are highly correlated, the model might give excessive importance to those
features, making it less generalized when applied to new data. Therefore,
identifying and removing highly correlated features can lead to a more robust and simpler model.

Moreover, correlation is essential for understanding relationships between
input features and target variables in predictive models. By analyzing correlation, one can determine which features are most influential in predicting
outcomes, enabling better model design.

Example

In machine learning, understanding correlation is very important when choosing which features to use in a model. Correlation shows how closely two variables are related. If two features are highly correlated, they often provide the same type of information. Keeping both in the model can be unnecessary and may cause the model to focus too much on them. This can lead to overfitting, where the model works well on training data but not on new data.

For example, imagine we are building a model to predict house prices. Two features in the dataset are square footage and number of bedrooms. These two features are often highly correlated because larger homes tend to have more bedrooms. Including both may not help the model, and could even confuse it. Instead, we might choose to keep just square footage or combine the two into a new feature, like square footage per bedroom. This makes the model simpler and helps it generalize better to new houses.

By using correlation to guide feature selection, we can build machine learning models that are more accurate, faster to train, and easier to understand.

Causality

Correlation shows how two variables move together, but it does not mean one causes the other. Causality, on the other hand, means that one variable directly influences another. Understanding causality is important in AI, especially for making informed decisions rather than just predicting outcomes.

Correlation vs. Causality

A common mistake in statistics and machine learning is assuming that correlation implies causation. For example, the number of ice cream sales and sunburn cases may be highly correlated, but eating ice cream doesn't cause sunburn both are influenced by hot weather. Correlation shows relationships, while causality identifies direct cause-and-effect links.

Knowing causal relationships helps improve decision-making. For example, a business analyzing a marketing campaign's effect on sales needs to determine whether the campaign actually caused increased sales or if other factors, like seasonal demand, played a role.

Causal Inference in AI

Most AI models rely on correlations, but causal inference aims to identify true cause-and-effect relationships. It uses methods like randomized controlled trials (RCTs), instrumental variables, and causal graphs. This helps AI systems provide better insights and simulate real-world scenarios more accurately.

Example

A company wants to know if its new marketing campaign actually boosted sales. After launching the campaign, sales went up. At first, this looks like a success. The company checks the data and sees a strong correlation between the campaign start and the sales increase—both happened around the same time. But they know correlation doesn't always mean one caused the other. For example, sales often rise during holidays, so the boost might be seasonal.

To find the real cause, the company uses a method called causal inference. They run a simple experiment: one group of customers sees the campaign, and another similar group does not. Both groups experience the same season, so the only major difference is the campaign. When the group that saw the campaign spends more, the company concludes the campaign truly caused the sales increase.

Now, with clear evidence, the company can plan future campaigns more wisely. This kind of thinking is key in AI and machine learning. Just because two things happen together doesn't mean one causes the other. AI systems must learn what truly drives change to help people make smarter, evidence-based decisions.

Review Questions

1. What does a correlation coefficient tell you about two variables?
2. What is the difference between Pearson's and Spearman's correlation?
3. How can correlation affect feature selection in machine learning?
4. What is the difference between correlation and causality?
5. Why is it important to understand causality in AI?
6. What methods are used for causal inference in AI?

3-4 Sampling and Sampling Distributions

Learning Outcomes

3-4-1 Understand how random sampling ensures fair data representation.

3-4-2 Learn how random sampling helps prevent overfitting.

3-4-3 Understand bootstrapping and how it improves model accuracy.

3-4-4 Know how bootstrapping is used in ensemble learning.

3-4-5 Learn how bootstrapping helps estimate data properties.

Random Sampling

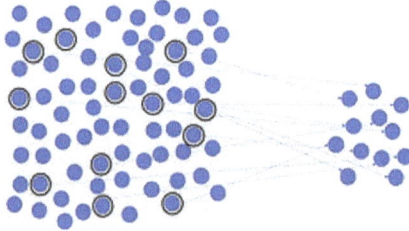

Random sampling is a fundamental technique in data science and machine learning that ensures every data point in a population has an equal chance of being selected. This helps create a dataset that accurately represents the larger population, allowing models to generalize well to unseen data. Without random sampling, there is a risk of bias, where certain groups or patterns may be overrepresented, leading to inaccurate predictions.

Preventing Overfitting

One important advantage of random sampling is that it helps prevent overfitting. Overfitting happens when a model learns patterns that are too specific to the training data, causing it to perform well there but poorly on new, unseen data. For instance, if a machine learning model predicting house prices is trained only on homes from one neighborhood, it might not do well when applied to other areas with different market trends. By using random sampling, the training data includes a wide range of examples from various locations, which makes the model more reliable and better at handling different situations.

Reducing Bias and Ensuring Fairness

Another major advantage of random sampling is its ability to reduce bias and promote fairness. If a dataset is not representative, a model may perform poorly when applied to different groups. For example, if a facial recognition system is trained primarily on images of people from one demographic, it may struggle with accurate predictions for individuals from other backgrounds. Random sampling helps address this problem by ensuring a fair distribution of data. This leads to more equitable and accurate machine learning models.

Example

A company wants to know if its new marketing campaign really helped increase sales. After launching the campaign, the company sees that sales have gone up. At first, this seems like a success. They check the data and notice a strong correlation between the campaign start date and the rise in sales. This means both events happened around the same time. But the company knows that correlation does not always mean one thing caused the other. For example, sales often go up during certain times of the year, like holidays. So, it's possible that the increase in sales was due to the season, not the campaign.

To find out the real reason, the company uses a method called causal inference. They set up a simple experiment called a randomized controlled trial. They show the marketing campaign to one group of customers, but not to another group that is similar in every other way. Both groups experience the same season, so the only big difference is whether they saw the marketing campaign. After comparing the two groups, the company sees that the group who got the marketing campaign spent more money. This shows that the campaign had a real effect on sales, not just the season.

Now that the company knows the campaign caused the increase, they can plan better in the future. They can use this knowledge to spend their marketing money more wisely and run campaigns at times when they know it will make a real difference. This kind of thinking is important in AI and machine learning. Just because two things happen at the same time doesn't mean one caused the other. AI systems need to understand not just what is related, but what truly causes change. This helps businesses, doctors, and other professionals make smarter choices based on real evidence.

Bootstrapping

Random sampling helps create a representative dataset, but bootstrapping takes resampling a step further to improve statistical estimates and model performance. Unlike random sampling, bootstrapping draws multiple samples from the same dataset with replacement, so some data points might appear more than once while others may be left out. By repeating this process many times, bootstrapping generates several new datasets that can be used to estimate statistics or train models more reliably and robustly.

Estimating Confidence Intervals and Model Reliability

Bootstrapping is particularly useful for estimating confidence intervals and measuring the reliability of a model's predictions. In cases where a fixed test set is unavailable or cross-validation is computationally expensive; bootstrapping provides an empirical method for assessing model performance. By resampling data multiple times and analyzing the variation in results, data scientists can gain a better understanding of how well a model is likely to perform on new data.

Approximating Statistical Properties

Bootstrapping also plays a crucial role in estimating statistical properties of a dataset. Since it allows for repeated sampling, it can be used to approximate the distribution of a given statistic, such as the mean or variance, even when working with small datasets. This makes bootstrapping a powerful tool for data scientists who need to make inferences from limited data.

Example

Estimating the Average Height of Students Using Bootstrapping

As a data analyst for a school, you are tasked with estimating the average height of all students, but you only have data from 50 students. To assess how confident you can be in your estimate for the entire school population of 1,000 students, you use bootstrapping, a technique that helps quantify uncertainty.

First, you calculate the mean height from the original dataset of 50 students. However, instead of relying solely on this sample, you apply bootstrapping. This involves resampling the original dataset multiple times (e.g., 1,000 times). Each resample, called a "bootstrap sample," is created by randomly selecting data points from the original dataset, allowing for repetition of some data points and exclusion of others.

For each of the 1,000 bootstrap samples, you compute the mean height. This results in 1,000 different estimates of the average height. By analyzing these estimates, you calculate the average of the 1,000 means, providing a more reliable estimate of the school population's true average height. Additionally, you can calculate the confidence interval, which shows the range of possible values for the true average height, using percentiles like the 5th and 95th percentiles.

Through bootstrapping, you gain a clearer understanding of the reliability of your estimate. The more times you resample, the more precise your estimate becomes, as you are not relying on a single sample but instead using multiple resamples to account for uncertainty. This method helps ensure your estimate reflects a range of possible outcomes, providing greater confidence in the result.

Review Questions

1. Why is random sampling important?
2. How does random sampling prevent overfitting?
3. What is bootstrapping and how does it help models?
4. How can bootstrapping estimate confidence intervals?
5. What is bagging, and how does bootstrapping help?

3-5 Predictive Modeling

Learning Outcomes

3-5-1 Understand linear regression and how it predicts continuous values.

3-5-2 Understand logistic regression and its use for binary classification.

3-5-3 Explain multiple regression and use of multiple factors to make predictions.

3-5-4 Identify real-world uses for linear, logistic, and multiple regression.

Regression models are fundamental tools for understanding relationships between variables and making predictions. These models serve as the foundation for many AI applications, helping to predict continuous outcomes, classify data, and handle more complex scenarios with multiple influencing factors. Among the most used regression techniques are linear regression, logistic regression, and multiple regression.

Types of Regression

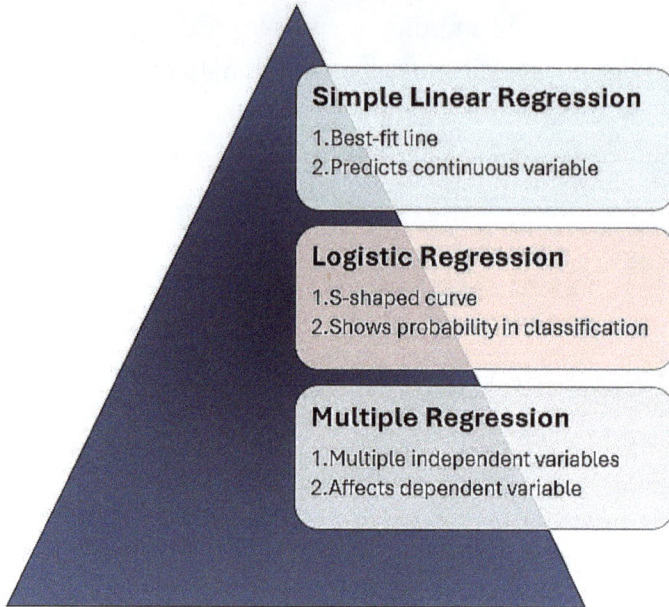

Simple Linear Regression

1. Best-fit line
2. Predicts continuous variable

Logistic Regression

1. S-shaped curve
2. Shows probability in classification

Multiple Regression

1. Multiple independent variables
2. Affects dependent variable

Linear Regression

Linear regression is one of the simplest and most widely used statistical techniques for predictive modeling. It is used to model the relationship between a dependent variable and one or more independent variables, under the assumption that this relationship is linear. In other words, linear regression assumes that changes in the independent variable(s) lead to proportional changes in the dependent variable.

How Linear Regression Works

In a typical linear regression model, the relationship between the dependent variable (the outcome we want to predict) and the independent variable(s) (the factors that influence the outcome) is expressed as a linear equation. The model aims to find the best-fitting line (in one dimension) or hyperplane (in multiple dimensions) that minimizes the difference between the observed data points and the predicted values.

This technique is especially useful when predicting continuous outcomes such as house prices, stock market trends, or temperature changes based on a set of known variables. For example, in predicting the price of a house, the independent variables might include features like the size of the house, the number of bedrooms, and the location, while the dependent variable would be the house price.

Applications of Linear Regression

Linear regression is frequently used in various AI and data science applications, especially when the goal is to predict continuous values. For example, it can be used for forecasting financial metrics, analyzing trends in sales data, or predicting the performance of a marketing campaign based on historical data.

Example

Imagine you are an AI data analyst working with a dataset of 100 employees. Each employee's years of experience and annual salary are recorded. The goal is to understand how years of experience affect salary and to build a model that predicts salary based on experience.

The foundation of simple linear regression is the equation of a straight line:

$y = mx + b$

In this equation, y represents the predicted salary, x is the number of years of experience, m is the slope of the line (which tells us how much salary increases for each additional year of experience), and b is the y-intercept, representing the salary when there are zero years of experience.

To build this model, you first train it using the data from the 100 employees. The model applies an algorithm called "least squares" to minimize the difference between the predicted salaries and the actual salaries in the dataset. By doing this, the model determines the best values for m and b. Once the model is trained, you can use it to make predictions.

For example, if the model computes that the slope (m) is 2000 and the intercept (b) is 30,000, the equation becomes:

Salary = 2000 × (Years of Experience) + 30000

If an employee has 5 years of experience, the model predicts their salary to be:

Salary = 2000 × 5 + 30000 = 40000

Logistic Regression

While linear regression is used for predicting continuous outcomes, logistic regression is employed for classification tasks, particularly when the outcome variable is categorical. Specifically, logistic regression is commonly used for binary classification, where the goal is to predict one of two possible outcomes, such as "yes" or "no," "spam" or "not spam," or "default" or "non-default."

How Logistic Regression Works

Unlike linear regression, which produces continuous output, logistic regression estimates the probability that a given input belongs to a certain class. It uses a logistic (or sigmoid) function to transform the predicted values into a probability range between 0 and 1. This transformation makes the model particularly suitable for classification tasks, as the output represents the likelihood of the input belonging to a certain class.

The output of logistic regression is a probability, which can be thresholded to make a final classification decision. For example, if the probability is greater than 0.5, the model classifies the input as "yes" (or the positive class), while if the probability is less than 0.5, it classifies it as "no" (or the negative class). The threshold of 0.5 is often used, but it can be adjusted depending on the specific problem and the trade-offs between false positives and false negatives.

Logistic regression is particularly effective because it transforms the output of linear regression into a form that is well-suited for classification problems. It is computationally efficient, easy to interpret, and can provide probabilities that give additional insight into the model's confidence in its predictions. Moreover, logistic regression serves as the foundation for more complex classification models, such as neural networks and support vector machines, which build upon similar principles but add more complexity and flexibility to handle non-linear relationships.

Applications of Logistic Regression

Logistic regression is widely used in AI applications where the objective is to classify data into one of two categories. Common use cases include spam detection, disease diagnosis (e.g., predicting whether a patient has a certain condition), and predicting customer churn in business applications. Its simplicity, interpretability, and efficiency make it a go-to model for binary classification problems.

Example

Logistic Regression for Spam Detection

An email service provider wants to classify emails as spam or not spam using logistic regression. The model uses features such as word frequency, presence of links, and sender reputation to predict whether an email is spam.

Logistic Regression Model

The model estimates the probability of an email being spam using the equation:

$$P(\text{spam}) = \frac{1}{1 + e^{-(\beta_0 + \beta_1 x_1 + \beta_2 x_2 + \cdots + \beta_n x_n)}}$$

where:

- $P(\text{spam})$ = probability that an email is spam

- β_0 = intercept

- $\beta_1, \beta_2, \ldots, \beta_n$ = coefficients for different email features

- $x_1, x_2, \ldots, x_n$ = feature values (e.g., number of suspicious words, presence of certain phrases)

If the model predicts P(spam) > 0.5, the email is classified as spam; otherwise, it is classified as not spam.

For example, an email with multiple links and suspicious words might have P(spam) = 0.85, meaning it is highly likely to be spam.

Multiple Regression

While linear regression is limited to predicting outcomes based on a single independent variable, multiple regression extends this idea to accommodate multiple independent variables. In multiple regression, the dependent variable is modeled as a linear combination of more than one independent variable. This makes multiple regression a more powerful tool for handling more complex datasets where multiple factors influence the outcome.

How Multiple Regression Works

In multiple regression, the relationship between the dependent variable and several independent variables is expressed as a linear equation involving multiple coefficients. The model seeks to find the best-fitting hyperplane that minimizes the sum of the squared residuals (the differences between observed and predicted values). By incorporating multiple predictors, multiple regression can capture more nuanced relationships between the dependent and independent variables.

Multiple regression is particularly useful when dealing with real-world scenarios where a single factor does not adequately explain the variability in the dependent variable. For example, predicting the price of a house would require considering several factors such as the size, location, and age of the house, along with economic factors like interest rates and market conditions.

Applications of Multiple Regression

Multiple regression is used in various fields where multiple factors influence an outcome. For instance, in economics, it can be applied to model GDP growth as a function of various economic indicators such as inflation, unemployment rate, and trade balances. In healthcare, multiple regression can help predict patient outcomes based on a variety of clinical and demographic variables. This technique is crucial for understanding complex, multi-factorial phenomena and making more accurate predictions.

Example

Multiple Regression for Predicting Machine Learning Model Performance

A data science team wants to predict the performance of a machine learning model based on various factors such as dataset size, number of features, and computational resources.

Multiple Regression Model

The relationship is modeled as:

$$y = \beta_0 + \beta_1 x_1 + \beta_2 x_2 + \beta_3 x_3 + \varepsilon$$

where:

-y = model accuracy (e.g., F1-score, precision, or recall)

-β_0 = intercept

-$\beta_1, \beta_2, \beta_3$ = coefficients for each independent variable

-x_1 = dataset size (number of samples)

-x_2 = number of features used

-x_3 = computational power (e.g., GPU cores used)

-ε = error term

Application

Using historical data from past experiments, the model estimates how these factors influence model accuracy. For example:

y = 50 + (0.05 × dataset size) + (0.2 × features) + (1.5 × GPU cores)

If a model is trained with:

- 10,000 samples

- 50 features

- 8 GPU cores

Then:

y = 50 + (0.05 × 10000) + (0.2 × 50) + (1.5 × 8) = 82

Multiple regression helps data scientists estimate machine learning model performance under different conditions, guiding decisions on dataset size, feature selection, and computational resources.

Review Questions

1. What is the main difference between linear regression and logistic regression?
2. Why use multiple regression instead of simple linear regression?
3. How does logistic regression turn numbers into probabilities?
4. What are some uses of linear regression?
5. When would you use logistic regression to classify things into two categories?
6. Why is multiple regression useful in predictions?

3-6 Hypothesis Testing and P-Values

Learning Outcomes

3-6-1 Understand the basics of hypothesis testing.
3-6-2 Interpret p-values.
3-6-3 Apply hypothesis testing to evaluate machine learning models.
3-6-4 Recognize the limitations of hypothesis testing.

In data science and machine learning, validating a model or measuring its performance often involves hypothesis testing. This statistical method helps determine whether an observed effect or relationship in the data is meaningful or just the result of random chance. Hypothesis testing is essential for data professionals, as it guides them in evaluating models and making better decisions. Understanding concepts like hypothesis testing and p-values is key for anyone working with data to ensure their findings are trustworthy and accurate.

What is Hypothesis Testing?

Hypothesis testing is a statistical procedure used to make inferences or draw conclusions about a population based on a sample of data. The process begins with the formulation of two competing hypotheses: the null hypothesis and the alternative hypothesis.

Null Hypothesis

The null hypothesis suggests that there is no effect or no difference in the data, or that any observed relationship is due to chance.

Alternative Hypothesis

The alternative hypothesis posits that there is an effect, relationship, or difference present in the data.

In machine learning, hypothesis testing is often used to evaluate whether a model's predictions are meaningful or if any observed patterns in the data are just the result of random fluctuations. For example, when comparing the performance of two machine learning models, a hypothesis test can help determine whether the observed difference in performance metrics (e.g., accuracy, F1 score) is statistically significant or whether it could have occurred by chance.

P-Values in Hypothesis Testing

One of the most important components of hypothesis testing is the p-value, a measure that helps determine the strength of the evidence against the null hypothesis. The p-value quantifies the probability of observing the test results, or more extreme outcomes, if the null hypothesis is true. Essentially, it helps answer the question: How likely is it that the observed data would occur if the null hypothesis were true?

The p-value is calculated based on the sample data and the statistical test being used. A smaller p-value indicates stronger evidence against the null hypothesis, suggesting that the observed effect or relationship is likely real and not due to random chance. Conversely, a larger p-value suggests weaker evidence against the null hypothesis, meaning that any observed effect may be the result of sampling variability rather than a true underlying relationship

Interpreting P-Values in Machine Learning

In machine learning, the p-value is commonly used when evaluating the significance of a model's performance or comparing different models. For example, when testing whether a new machine learning model performs significantly better than an existing model, hypothesis testing can help determine whether the improvement is statistically significant. Here, the p-value helps data scientists assess if the observed improvement in accuracy, precision, recall, or other performance metrics is likely to be due to the new model's ability to generalize well, or if it could just be a random fluctuation.

Typically, a significance level (denoted as alpha) is chosen before conducting the hypothesis test. This threshold determines the probability at which the null hypothesis is rejected. A common significance level used in many statistical tests is 0.05, meaning that the results are considered statistically significant if the p-value is less than 0.05.

If p-value < 0.05

This suggests that the results are statistically significant, and the null hypothesis can be rejected. In the context of machine learning, this might mean that a model's performance improvement is unlikely to be due to chance.

If p-value > 0.05

This suggests that the results are not statistically significant, and the null hypothesis cannot be rejected. In the machine learning context, this might mean that the difference in performance between two models is likely due to random variability rather than a true difference in their effectiveness.

Using Hypothesis Testing in Model Evaluation

Hypothesis testing is an important tool for evaluating machine learning models, particularly when comparing different models or algorithms. For example, when selecting between a decision tree model and a support vector machine, hypothesis testing can help determine whether one model significantly outperforms the other in terms of prediction accuracy. Additionally, hypothesis tests can help assess whether improvements made to an existing model (e.g., hyperparameter tuning or feature engineering) lead to statistically significant gains in performance.

By using hypothesis testing in model evaluation, machine learning practitioners can avoid making false conclusions based on noise in the data. This ensures that only truly effective models or techniques are adopted, leading to more reliable and valid predictions.

Limitations and Considerations

While hypothesis testing and p-values are powerful tools, they have some limitations, particularly in the context of machine learning:

P-Value Misinterpretation

A small p-value does not necessarily imply a strong or practically meaningful effect. It merely indicates that the observed effect is unlikely to be due to chance. Practitioners should also consider the effect size, context of the problem, and other performance metrics when interpreting p-values.

Multiple Testing Problem

When conducting multiple hypothesis tests (e.g., when comparing many different models), the chance of observing a significant result purely by chance increases. Adjustments such as the Bonferroni correction can help address this issue.

Overfitting Risk

A statistically significant result does not necessarily mean that the model is generalizable. Machine learning models can still be overfit to training data, leading to poor performance on unseen data even if their p-values indicate statistical significance.

Thus, while hypothesis testing and p-values are important tools for model evaluation, they should be used in conjunction with other techniques such as cross-validation, domain knowledge, and model performance metrics to ensure the robustness and generalizability of machine learning models.

Example

Hypothesis Testing in Machine Learning

An e-commerce company tests a new recommendation model (Model B) against the current model (Model A) using click-through rate (CTR) as the key metric.

Hypothesis Setup

- Null Hypothesis (H_0): No significant difference in CTR between Model A and Model B.

- Alternative Hypothesis (H_1): Model B has a significantly higher CTR.

 Experiment and Results - Model A CTR: 5.2

- Model B CTR: 5.8

- Sample Size: 100,000 recommendations per model

- p-value: 0.03 (alpha = 0.05)

Since $p < 0.05$, the null hypothesis is rejected, showing Model B's improvement is statistically significant.

Conclusion

Model B is recommended for deployment, but further validation is needed to confirm effectiveness across different users.

Review Questions

1. What is the difference between the null hypothesis and the alternative hypothesis?
2. What does a small p-value indicate in hypothesis testing?
3. When is a result considered statistically significant in hypothesis testing?
4. Why is hypothesis testing important in evaluating machine learning models?
5. What are some limitations of using p-values in hypothesis testing?
6. What should you consider along with p-values when evaluating a model's performance?

Chapter 4

Data Wrangling

Data wrangling is the process of transforming and cleaning raw data into a usable format for analysis.

Before data can be analyzed, it must be prepared properly. Data preparation is essential because raw data is often messy, inconsistent, and incomplete. The process of wrangling and preparing data ensures that the dataset is clean, structured, and formatted appropriately for analysis. Without proper preparation, data analysis can lead to misleading conclusions and incorrect predictions.

Data preparation is a time-consuming but necessary part of any data project. It typically involves removing errors, handling missing values, and organizing data in a manner that supports effective analysis. By investing in good data preparation, organizations can ensure their analysis is accurate and meaningful. For example, businesses might prepare their data to forecast trends in sales or assess customer satisfaction based on historical data.

4-1 Data Cleaning Techniques

Learning Outcomes

4-1-1 Handle missing data using imputation, removal, or prediction.
4-1-2 Remove duplicate data to ensure accurate results.
4-1-3 Identify and deal with outliers.
4-1-4 Standardize data formats and types for consistency.
4-1-5 Understand how data cleaning improves analysis.

Data cleaning is a vital part of the data wrangling process. It involves fixing problems like missing values, duplicate records, inconsistencies, and incorrect data types. Since the quality of data directly affects how accurate and reliable the analysis will be, cleaning is a necessary step before any meaningful insights can be drawn. Well-cleaned data helps ensure that the conclusions and decisions based on it are trustworthy and useful.

Handling Missing Data

Options to Handle Missing Data

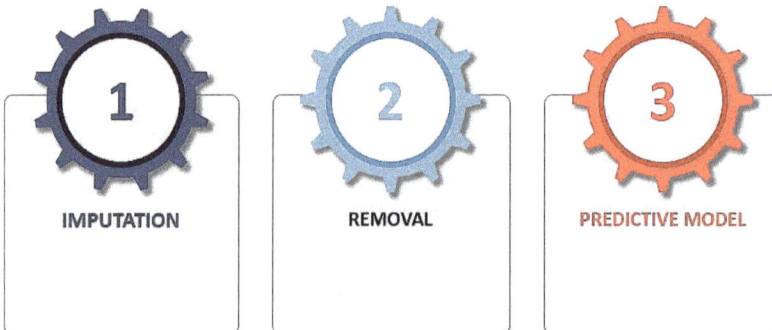

1 IMPUTATION

2 REMOVAL

3 PREDICTIVE MODEL

One of the most common challenges faced during data cleaning is handling missing data. Missing values can arise due to several reasons, such as incomplete surveys, system errors, or issues during data collection. When datasets contain missing values, they can lead to biased or incomplete results, which can significantly affect the outcomes of analysis.

There are several strategies for addressing missing data, each suited to different situations.

Imputation

This involves replacing missing values with estimated values. The missing data can be filled with the mean, median, or mode of the column, depending on the data distribution. Imputation helps maintain the integrity of the dataset by ensuring that the missing values do not disrupt analysis, though it is essential to consider the impact of the imputed values on the overall analysis.

Example

Scenario: The age column has missing values for a couple of employees.

Approach: To fill these gaps, you decide to use imputation. You calculate the mean age of all the employees who have a recorded age and then use this mean to fill in the missing values. Outcome: The missing age values are replaced with the calculated average, ensuring that the dataset remains intact without dropping any data.

Removal

In some cases, removing rows or columns with missing data may be the best approach, especially if the missing values are in non-essential variables or if a large portion of the dataset is affected. However, this method can lead to the loss of valuable information, so it should be used cautiously.

> **Example**
>
> Scenario: The salary column has missing values, and these missing values are spread across multiple rows.
>
> Approach: In this case, you might choose to use the removal method. If the missing salary values are not too many and the rows with missing data don't contain crucial information, you can remove the rows with missing salary data entirely. This avoids making assumptions about those missing values but results in losing some data.
>
> Outcome: The dataset is reduced, but you retain only rows with complete information, which might be important for your analysis.

Predictive Models

For more advanced situations, missing values can be estimated using predictive algorithms. These models use other available data to estimate the missing values, providing a more sophisticated way to handle missing data, especially when the data has complex relationships.

Choosing the right approach for handling missing data depends on the nature of the dataset, the amount of missing data, and the goals of the analysis. Each method has its trade-offs, and analysts must carefully consider the implications of each choice.

> **Example**
>
> Scenario: Some salaries are missing, but you suspect there might be a relationship between salary and age.
>
> Approach: Instead of simply imputing or removing the missing values, you could use predictive models. For example, you can use a regression model where age is used to predict salary. Using this model, you estimate the missing salary values based on the age of each employee.
>
> Outcome: The missing salary values are predicted using the relationship between age and salary, allowing you to preserve the integrity of the data without losing any information.

Dealing with Duplicates and Outliers

Duplicates

Duplicate data entries are another common issue in data cleaning. Duplicates can arise when the same data is recorded more than once, either due to system errors or repeated data collection. If left unchecked, duplicates can distort the results of data analysis, leading to overestimation or underestimation of trends and patterns.

To maintain data integrity, it is essential to identify and remove duplicates. Removing duplicates ensures that the analysis is based on unique and accurate data points, preventing skewed results and improving the overall reliability of the dataset.

> **Example**
>
> E-commerce customer records
>
> An online store collects customer purchase data. Due to a system glitch, some customers' orders are recorded twice.
>
> AI deduplication models compare customer names, email addresses, and purchase timestamps to identify and merge duplicate entries.
>
> This prevents inflated sales numbers and ensures accurate customer insights

Outliers

Outliers are extreme values that differ significantly from the rest of the data. While outliers may indicate errors or anomalies in the dataset, they can also reflect rare but legitimate occurrences. For instance, an outlier in a dataset of ages might be a data entry error, such as a person mistakenly recorded as being 200 years old. However, in other cases, outliers may represent significant data points that offer valuable insights, such as a rare disease or an unusual market trend.

Handling outliers requires careful consideration. Analysts can use statistical methods, such as calculating Z-scores or interquartile range (IQR), to identify data points that fall outside the typical range. Visualization tools like box plots or scatter plots can also help in visually identifying outliers. Once identified, analysts must decide whether to remove, adjust, or retain outliers based on their understanding of the data and the context of the analysis.

> **Example**
>
> Fraud detection in banking
>
> A bank analyzes transaction amounts to detect anomalies. Most transactions fall within a normal range, but some are significantly high or low.
>
> AI-powered anomaly detection models (like Isolation Forest or Autoencoders) flag transactions that deviate from usual spending patterns.
>
> Analysts then review flagged transactions to distinguish fraud from legitimate high-value transactions.

Standardizing Formats and Data Types

Standardization is another important aspect of data cleaning. When working with datasets, it is essential to ensure that data is consistent in terms of format and data types. Inconsistent data formats or incorrect data types can lead to errors during analysis, as well as confusion when performing calculations or merging datasets.

For example, date formats may vary between "MM/DD/YYYY" or "DD-MM-YYYY," leading to potential misinterpretation of the data. Standardizing the date format across the entire dataset ensures that dates are properly interpreted and can be compared and analyzed without issues. Similarly, numerical data should be stored in consistent formats, such as integers or floats, rather than strings, to ensure accurate calculations.

Standardizing formats and data types helps ensure that the dataset is uniform, making it easier to perform operations and analyses. This step is particularly important when combining datasets from multiple sources, as each source may have different conventions for representing the same type of data.

Data Type	Inconsistent Format	Standardized Format
Dates	03/25/2025, 25-03-2025, March 25, 2025	2025-03-25 (YYYY-MM-DD)
Phone Numbers	+1 (555) 123-4567, 555.123.4567, 555-123-4567	+1-555-123-4567
Addresses	123 Main St., 123 Main Street, 123 MAIN ST	123 Main Street
Boolean Values	Yes/No, True/False, 1/0, Y/N	True/False
Currencies	$100, 100 USD, 100.00	100.00 USD
Categorical Data	Male/Female, M/F, man/woman	Male/Female
Timestamps	03/25/2025 5:30 PM, 2025-03-25T17:30:00Z	2025-03-25 17:30:00 (UTC

Review Questions

1. How can you handle missing data?
2. Why is it important to remove duplicates from your data?
3. What are outliers, and how should you deal with them?
4. Why is it necessary to standardize data formats and types?
5. Why remove data instead of filling in missing values?

4-2 Data Importing and Exporting

Learning Outcomes

4-2-1 Import and export data from CSV, Excel, and JSON files.
4-2-2 Understand when to use CSV, Excel, or JSON files.
4-2-3 Connect to a relational database and get data.
4-2-4 Know the benefits of using databases for data management.

Efficient data wrangling goes beyond cleaning and manipulating data; it also requires the ability to import data from various sources and export cleaned datasets into different formats for further analysis, sharing, or collaboration. Being able to work with diverse file types and connect to databases is essential for data professionals, ensuring that they can handle a wide range of data sources and formats. This process involves reading from and writing to various file types, such as CSV, Excel, and JSON files, and connecting to relational databases for querying and retrieving data.

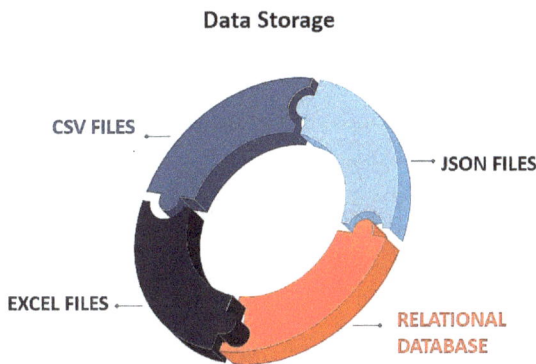

Data Storage

CSV FILES

JSON FILES

EXCEL FILES

RELATIONAL DATABASE

Reading and Writing Files

CSV Files

Comma-separated values (CSV) files are one of the most widely used formats for storing tabular data. These files contain rows of data with each value separated by commas, making them simple and accessible for analysis. CSV files are often preferred because of their ease of use, portability, and compatibility with most data analysis tools. However, they may not be as efficient for storing large datasets due to their lack of data compression and support for complex data types. Despite these limitations, CSV files remain an essential format for analysts, as they can easily be imported into analysis environments and shared across different platforms.

Excel Files

Excel files, particularly in the .xlsx or .xls formats, are commonly used in business environments for storing and manipulating data. Excel files are popular because they provide a user-friendly interface for data entry and analysis, making them ideal for both technical and non-technical users. Excel files often contain multiple sheets, which can hold different datasets related to one another. For data analysts, the ability to read and write Excel files programmatically is critical, as it allows seamless integration of spreadsheets into automated analysis workflows. Tools such as Python libraries and R packages provide functions to handle these file formats, enabling analysts to work directly with data stored in Excel files in their coding environment.

JSON Files

JavaScript Object Notation (JSON) files are used for storing hierarchical or nested data. JSON is a lightweight data-interchange format that is particularly suited for complex data structures, making it a popular choice for web applications and APIs. Unlike CSV or Excel files, JSON can store nested data in the form of arrays and objects, making it ideal for data that involves multiple layers of information, such as user profiles, transactions, or sensor data. JSON is commonly used in applications where data is transferred between servers and clients in a web environment. Data analysts can use various libraries to read and write JSON files, making it easier to handle this flexible format for analysis.

Connecting to Databases for Data Import

Relational Databases

Many organizations store their data in relational databases such as MySQL, PostgreSQL, or SQL Server. These databases allow for efficient data storage and retrieval, particularly for large datasets that would be cumbersome to manage in flat file formats like CSV or Excel. Data wrangling often involves connecting to these databases to query data and bringing it into analysis environments for further processing.

Tools for Database Connectivity

To connect to relational databases, analysts often use tools like Python s SQL Alchemy or R s DBI package. These libraries provide the necessary functionality to interact with databases, execute SQL queries, and import the data directly into programming environments. This allows for more efficient handling of large datasets, as databases are optimized for querying and managing data, unlike flat files, which may become slow and inefficient with larger volumes of information.

Advantages of Databases

Connecting to databases offers several advantages for data wrangling. Databases allow for better organization, querying, and storage of data, making them more suitable for working with large datasets compared to flat files. They also provide more robust data integrity, allowing for easier management of relationships between tables and access control. By using a database management system (DBMS), analysts can directly query data in a more structured and efficient manner, which streamlines the wrangling process and makes it easier to work with real-time data.

Review Questions

1. What is the difference between CSV and Excel files?
2. When would you use a JSON file?
3. How can you get data from a database?
4. Why are databases better than flat files for large data?
5. Why is it important to export data in different formats?

4-3 Data Transformation and Manipulation

Learning Outcomes

4-3-1 Filter data based on specific conditions.
4-3-2 Sort data in order to find patterns.
4-3-3 Summarize data using basic aggregation.
4-3-4 Combine data from different sources.
4-3-5 Select specific data to focus on.

Once data has been cleaned and imported, the next critical step in the data wrangling process is transforming and manipulating the data. Data transformation and manipulation involve various operations designed to organize and refine data, making it ready for in-depth analysis. These steps typically include filtering, sorting, aggregating, joining, merging, and subsetting data. These techniques help streamline datasets, identify patterns, and make data more manageable, ultimately enabling more effective decision-making.

Filtering, Sorting, and Aggregating Data

Filtering Data

Filtering is often one of the initial steps in working with data, allowing analysts to pull out specific portions of the dataset based on set criteria. This helps focus the analysis on the most relevant information, making the process more efficient. For example, in a sales dataset, filtering might be used to select transactions from the last month or to focus on customers from a certain region. By narrowing down the data this way, analysts can make sure their insights are based on the most meaningful and targeted information.

Sorting Data

Sorting is a basic but important part of working with data. It arranges information in a specific order—either ascending or descending—based on one or more variables. Sorting helps organize data so that patterns and trends become clearer. For example, sorting products by price or sales by volume can help analysts quickly spot the best-selling items or top-performing categories. Using sorting techniques makes data easier to explore and supports smarter decision-making.

Aggregating Data

Aggregation involves summarizing data to provide a high-level overview of key metrics. Analysts use aggregation to compute values such as averages, sums, counts, or medians within defined groups. For example, sales data can be aggregated by the region to find the total sales in each area. This technique helps analysts identify broader trends, such as which regions are performing better, or which time periods have the highest sales. Aggregation is particularly useful when working with large datasets, as it allows analysts to focus on summarized results rather than individual data points.

Joining, Merging, and Subsetting Data

Joining and Merging Data

Data often exists across multiple tables or datasets, and combining these datasets is a critical part of the analysis process. Joining and merging are techniques used to link datasets based on common keys or identifiers. These operations are vital in relational databases, where information is typically stored in separate tables that need to be brought together to provide a complete picture.

Joining data allows analysts to combine rows from two or more datasets where there is a match between specific columns, such as customer IDs or product identifiers. Merging data can involve different types of joins, such as inner joins, left joins, and outer joins, depending on the desired outcome. The key to successful joining and merging is ensuring that the datasets share a common identifier that links them logically. This enables analysts to analyze relationships across multiple data sources, such as linking customer information with sales transactions to better understand customer behavior.

Subsetting Data

Subsetting is a technique used to extract specific rows or columns from a dataset that are relevant to the analysis. This operation is particularly useful when working with large datasets, where only a portion of the data is necessary for the task at hand. By subsetting data, analysts can remove irrelevant information and focus only on the most critical data points.

For instance, if a dataset contains customer information for various regions but the analysis is focused only on one region, subsetting allows the analyst to isolate just the data for that region. Similarly, analysts might choose to subset the dataset by selecting only the columns that are necessary for a specific analysis, streamlining the data and making the process more efficient.

4-4 Introduction to SQL

SQL (Structured Query Language) is a powerful language used for managing and querying relational databases. It is a fundamental tool for data wrangling and is essential for working with large datasets stored in relational databases. SQL provides users with a flexible and efficient way to retrieve, modify, and manipulate data in a database, enabling data analysts and data scientists to process data and extract valuable insights.

Basic Queries in SQL

One of the most fundamental aspects of SQL is the ability to perform basic queries to retrieve data from a database. A basic query allows users to select specific columns from one or more tables, apply conditions, and filter the dataset as needed. The general syntax of a SQL query is as follows:

SELECT column1, column2

FROM table

WHERE condition;

This query selects the specified columns (column1, column2) from the specified table (table) where the provided condition is met. The WHERE clause filters the data based on the condition, ensuring that only the rows that meet the criteria are returned.

Example

To retrieve the names and ages of employees who are over 30 years old, the query would look like:

SELECT name, age

FROM employees

WHERE age > 30;

Basic SQL queries are essential for performing simple data retrieval tasks, and they serve as the foundation for more complex operations.

Table Joins in SQL

Types of Joins

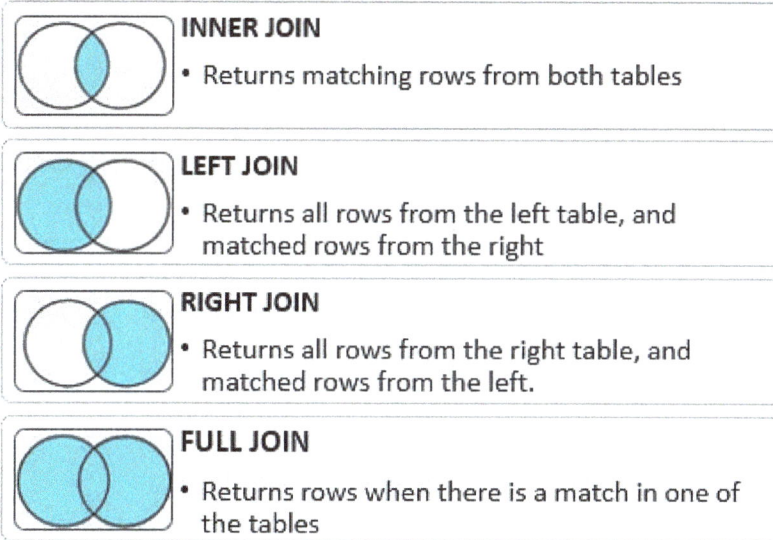

INNER JOIN
- Returns matching rows from both tables

LEFT JOIN
- Returns all rows from the left table, and matched rows from the right

RIGHT JOIN
- Returns all rows from the right table, and matched rows from the left.

FULL JOIN
- Returns rows when there is a match in one of the tables

While basic queries allow users to extract data from a single table, data often resides in multiple tables in a relational database. In such cases, SQL provides the ability to combine data from different tables using joins. A join is a method used to link data from two or more tables based on a common key, such as an ID or another shared attribute.

There are different types of joins in SQL, with the most commonly used being INNER JOIN, LEFT JOIN, RIGHT JOIN, and FULL JOIN. Here, we will focus on a basic INNER JOIN, which combines rows from both tables where there is a match in the specified key.

Suppose we have two tables: customers and sales. The customers table contains customer information (e.g., customer_id, name), and the sales table contains sales transaction details (e.g., transaction_id, customer_id, amount). To analyze customer behavior, we might want to combine data from both tables using the common key customer_id:

```
SELECT customers.name, sales.amount FROM customers JOIN sales ON
customers.customer_id = sales.customer_id;
```

This query selects the name from the customers table and the amount from the sales table, linking the two tables using the customer_id column. The JOIN keyword ensures that only rows where there is a matching customer_id in both tables are included in the result set.

Table joins are vital for extracting meaningful insights from relational databases, as data is often spread across multiple tables and requires joining to gain a complete understanding.

Filtering Data in SQL

In addition to joining tables, filtering data is an important feature of SQL. The WHERE clause allows users to apply conditions to filter the dataset, ensuring that only relevant data is included in the query results. By using conditions such as equality (=), inequality (!=), range (BETWEEN), and pattern matching (LIKE), SQL users can tailor their queries to return exactly the data they need.

Suppose we want to find the sales transactions for customers who made purchases over $100. The query would look like this:

```
SELECT customers.name, sales.amount FROM customers JOIN sales ON
customers.customer_id = sales.customer_id WHERE sales.amount >
100;
```

In this query, the WHERE clause filters the results to include only those transactions where the amount is greater than 100. This filtering capability is essential for narrowing down large datasets to focus on specific subsets of data.

Advanced

SQL also supports more advanced filtering techniques, such as AND and OR operators, which allow users to combine multiple conditions in a single query.

This query retrieves sales transactions over $100 for customers who are located in New York. By combining conditions, SQL users can filter data based on multiple criteria to produce more targeted and meaningful results.

```
SELECT customers.name, sales.amount FROM customers JOIN sales ON
customers.customer_id = sales.customer_id WHERE sales.amount >
100 AND customers.city = 'New York';
```

Review Questions

1. What is SQL and why is it important?
2. What is the purpose of the SELECT statement in SQL?
3. How do you perform a table join in SQL?
4. What is the difference between INNER JOIN and other types of joins?
5. How can you filter data in SQL using the WHERE clause?
6. What is the purpose of using AND and OR operators in SQL queries?

Chapter 5

Data Mining

5-1 Overview

Learning Outcomes
5-1-1 Understand what data mining is and why it's important.
5-1-2 Describe the main steps in data mining.
5-1-3 Explain how to evaluate the usefulness of patterns found in data.
5-1-4 Recognize real-world uses of data mining.
5-1-5 Understand how data mining helps businesses make better decisions.

Data mining is the process of extracting valuable knowledge from vast amounts of raw data. By discovering hidden patterns, trends, and relationships, data mining helps organizations turn their data into actionable insights that can enhance decision-making, improve efficiency, and optimize operations. In this section, we will explore the process of data mining and examine how it is applied in various real-world contexts.

Discovering Patterns in Data

The goal of data mining is to uncover patterns within large datasets that can inform decision-making and support business or operational objectives. The data mining process typically involves several key stages: data collection, data cleaning and preprocessing, data exploration, pattern recognition, and evaluation and interpretation. These steps are essential to ensure that the data used for analysis is accurate, meaningful, and relevant.

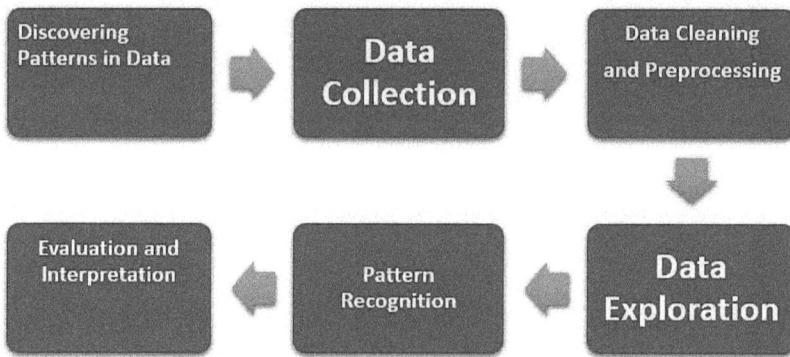

Data Collection

The first step in the data mining process is gathering relevant data from a variety of sources. This data can come from databases, online platforms, sensors, or external data providers. The quality and diversity of the data collected are critical for ensuring that the insights derived from the mining process are comprehensive and representative.

Data Cleaning and Preprocessing

Raw data often comes with imperfections, such as missing values, inconsistencies, or duplicates. Data cleaning is a vital step that involves addressing

118

these issues to prepare the data for analysis. Preprocessing also includes transforming data into a suitable format, normalizing values, and removing irrelevant information. Clean and well-prepared data is essential for ensuring that the analysis is accurate, and the results are reliable.

Data Exploration

After the data has been cleaned and preprocessed, the next step is to explore the data. This involves summarizing and visualizing the data to understand its structure and distribution. Data exploration helps identify potential relationships or patterns within the data that may not be immediately apparent. Techniques like descriptive statistics and data visualization tools, such as histograms, scatter plots, and heat maps, are often used in this stage to gain initial insights.

Pattern Recognition

Once the data is prepared and explored, data mining techniques such as classification, regression, and clustering are applied to recognize patterns and trends. This stage involves using algorithms to model data and identify meaningful relationships. For instance, classification algorithms may group data into categories, while regression techniques predict continuous outcomes. Clustering algorithms, on the other hand, group similar data points together, revealing hidden structures or segments in the data.

Evaluation and Interpretation

The final step of the data mining process involves evaluating the patterns discovered during analysis to ensure that they are valid, meaningful, and useful. This is a critical step, as not all patterns uncovered by mining techniques will be relevant or actionable. Once valid patterns are identified, they can be used to make predictions, inform decisions, or drive business strategies. For example, a retail company might use data mining to predict future sales trends, while a healthcare organization might identify high-risk patients based on historical data.

Example

In the competitive retail landscape, understanding customer behavior is vital. FreshMart, a mid-sized retail chain, faced a recurring problem: frequent stockouts of popular items in some stores and excessive inventory in others. Traditional forecasting methods failed to capture these nuances, prompting the company to embrace data mining as a strategic solution.

FreshMart collected one year of transaction data from both online and physical stores, including purchase histories, customer demographics, weather patterns, local events, and in-store navigation data from heat sensors. After cleaning and standardizing the dataset, the team applied several data mining techniques to uncover actionable insights.

Using association rule mining, they found that fresh bread purchases often coincided with cheese and wine—leading to a bundled promotion that boosted sales by 18 percent. Clustering analysis revealed three key customer segments: "Weekend Shoppers," "Health Enthusiasts," and "Discount Hunters." This segmentation allowed for targeted marketing, increasing email campaign response rates by 22 percent.

Through predictive modeling with decision trees, the company forecasted product demand with greater precision. For example, bottled water sales were predicted to spike during heatwaves, enabling preemptive restocking and reducing missed sales opportunities.

By leveraging data mining, FreshMart transformed its inventory planning, reduced waste, and enhanced customer satisfaction—demonstrating the power of data-driven retail strategy

---

The end goal of data mining is to produce actionable insights that can improve business strategies, operations, and outcomes. These insights can drive decision-making across various sectors, from marketing and customer relationship management to inventory management and fraud detection.

Real-World Applications

Data mining has a broad range of applications across different industries and sectors. It is used to gain insights, enhance decision-making, and drive improvements in both operational efficiency and customer experience. Below are some key areas where data mining plays a crucial role:

Customer Relationship Management (CRM)

Data mining is extensively used in customer relationship management to understand customer behavior, preferences, and purchasing patterns. By analyzing historical data, businesses can identify which products or services are likely to attract specific customer segments. This allows companies to tailor marketing strategies, personalize promotions, and ultimately improve customer retention and satisfaction. For example, e-commerce platforms use data mining to recommend products based on previous customer purchases, increasing the likelihood of future sales.

Example

ShopSmart, a growing e-commerce platform, struggled with low customer retention and ineffective marketing. Despite attracting a large customer base, many users were infrequent shoppers, and the lack of relevant product recommendations led to missed revenue opportunities. To address these issues, ShopSmart turned to data mining to better understand customer behavior and optimize its marketing efforts.

The company began by analyzing purchase histories and browsing patterns. This revealed that customers who bought electronics often returned shortly after to purchase related accessories. By leveraging this insight, ShopSmart introduced targeted product recommendations, resulting in a 15 percent sales increase in accessories.

Next, ShopSmart focused on personalized promotions. Data mining showed that loyal customers were more likely to respond to exclusive discounts tailored to their interests. Acting on this, the company launched individualized email campaigns featuring previously viewed or related items. This boosted conversion rates by 20 percent.

Further segmentation of the customer base revealed distinct groups: budget shoppers, tech enthusiasts, and fashion-forward buyers. Customized marketing campaigns were crafted for each segment, enhancing engagement and improving customer retention by 18 percent.

Finally, ShopSmart refined its product recommendation engine. By analyzing customers' prior purchases and browsing habits, the platform recommended complementary and similar items, leading to a 25 percent increase in cross-selling and upselling.

Through strategic use of data mining, ShopSmart transformed its customer experience, significantly improving sales, retention, and marketing effectiveness.

Healthcare

In healthcare, data mining is an important tool for enhancing patient care and managing health outcomes. By analyzing medical records, hospitals can forecast disease outbreaks, pinpoint patients at high risk, and tailor treatment plans to individual needs. Data mining also supports better hospital operations by predicting patient admissions and improving inventory management. Furthermore, healthcare professionals use these techniques to uncover patterns in how diseases progress, helping to shape preventive care strategies and ultimately improve patient health.

Example

HealthFirst Medical Center, a large hospital system, faced mounting challenges with high patient readmission rates, escalating operational costs, and a growing need to personalize care. In response, the hospital adopted data mining techniques to better understand patient patterns, optimize operations, and improve treatment outcomes.

One of the key breakthroughs came from predicting disease outbreaks. By analyzing historical patient records alongside external factors like weather patterns, HealthFirst was able to forecast seasonal illnesses such as the flu. This allowed the hospital to implement preventive care campaigns and stock essential medications in advance, resulting in a 30 percent decrease in flu-related hospital admissions.

Another major focus was identifying high-risk patients. Using data mining to examine chronic disease profiles, the hospital pinpointed individuals most likely to be readmitted due to conditions such as heart disease and diabetes. By providing targeted follow-up care and early intervention, HealthFirst successfully reduced readmission rates by 25 percent.

In terms of operational efficiency, data mining revealed patterns in patient admissions based on frequency and seasonal trends. This insight enabled more accurate staffing schedules and better inventory planning, leading to a 15 percent reduction in operational costs annually.

Finally, the hospital used data to develop personalized treatment plans. By studying disease progression and treatment responses across patient groups, physicians identified the most effective regimens for managing chronic conditions. These customized plans improved patient outcomes, with a 20 percent boost in treatment effectiveness.

Through data mining, HealthFirst Medical Center not only enhanced patient care but also improved efficiency and reduced costs—

demonstrating the critical role of data in modern healthcare.

Finance

The finance industry depends heavily on data mining for tasks like assessing risk, detecting fraud, and forecasting market trends. For example, banks and financial institutions analyze transaction data with data mining algorithms to spot unusual activity that could signal fraud. Credit scoring models use these techniques to evaluate the creditworthiness of individuals and businesses. Additionally, financial analysts apply data mining to predict stock market movements and help guide smarter investment decisions.

Example

SecureBank, a major financial institution, faced growing challenges in combating fraud and improving its risk assessment strategies. With the rise of complex financial crimes and the limitations of traditional credit evaluation methods, the bank turned to data mining to enhance security, improve lending decisions, and forecast market trends more accurately.

One of the most urgent problems was fraud detection. By analyzing transaction data, data mining algorithms flagged suspicious behavior, such as rapid withdrawals from multiple locations. In response, Secure-Bank developed a real-time alert system that monitored these patterns and automatically blocked questionable transactions. This proactive approach led to a 40 percent reduction in fraud.

The bank also aimed to improve its credit scoring process. Traditional credit reports were limited in scope, often overlooking valuable behavioral data. By incorporating customers' transaction histories and spending habits, SecureBank developed a more nuanced credit scoring model. This allowed the bank to identify creditworthy individuals who might have been rejected under old models. As a result, loan approvals increased by 10 percent without raising default rates.

Beyond individual banking, SecureBank applied data mining to market trend forecasting. Analysts studied historical stock performance in relation to economic indicators such as interest rates and market sentiment. These insights enabled more accurate predictions of stock movements, improving investment strategies and boosting portfolio returns by 15 percent.

By integrating data mining into its operations, SecureBank significantly strengthened its fraud prevention, expanded access to credit, and enhanced its investment decision-making—demonstrating the power of data-driven finance.

Retail

Retailers leverage data mining to better understand customer shopping patterns and fine-tune their product offerings. By examining transaction data, they can spot buying trends, recognize seasonal shifts, and group customers based on their purchasing habits. This insight helps improve inventory management, adjust pricing strategies, and boost the impact of marketing campaigns. Additionally, data mining enables retailers to personalize shopping experiences, like recommending products tailored to a customer's past purchases or browsing behavior.

Review Questions

1. What is data mining and why is it important?
2. What are the main steps in data mining?
3. Why do we need to clean and prepare data before analyzing it?
4. What are some ways to explore data and understand it?
5. How does data mining help businesses understand their customers better?
6. How can data mining help doctors and hospitals improve patient care?
7. How do banks use data mining to find fraud and assess risk?

5-2 Data Mining Algorithms

Learning Outcomes

5-2-1 Understand the difference between supervised and unsupervised learning.

5-2-2 Describe classification and regression algorithms.

5-2-3 Explain how classification algorithms work.

5-2-4 Understand basic regression types.

5-2-5 Know the key clustering methods.

5-2-6 Identify when to use each algorithm.

Data mining algorithms are the backbone of the data analysis process, helping to extract meaningful patterns and insights from large datasets. These algorithms are fundamental for tasks such as classification, prediction, and clustering. A clear understanding of these algorithms is essential for anyone working in data science, analytics, or machine learning. In this section, we will explore two major categories of data mining algorithms: classification and regression, as well as clustering techniques. These algorithms allow data scientists to tackle a variety of real-world problems across different industries.

Classification and regression are two essential types of supervised learning algorithms. Supervised learning refers to the use of labeled data, where the desired output (the target variable) is known, and the algorithm learns to make predictions or classify data based on these known labels.

Classification Algorithms

The primary goal of classification algorithms is to categorize data into predefined classes or groups. These algorithms are used when the output is a discrete label. A classic example is spam email classification, where the task is to classify an email as either "spam" or "not spam" based on certain features such as sender, subject, and content.

Classification Algorithms

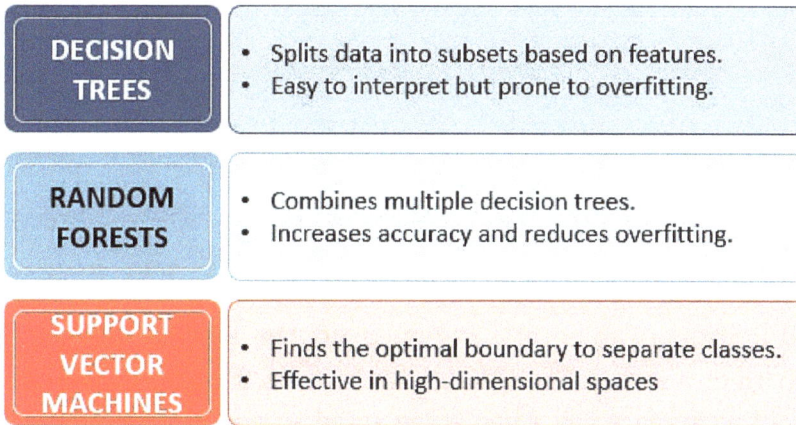

DECISION TREES	• Splits data into subsets based on features. • Easy to interpret but prone to overfitting.
RANDOM FORESTS	• Combines multiple decision trees. • Increases accuracy and reduces overfitting.
SUPPORT VECTOR MACHINES	• Finds the optimal boundary to separate classes. • Effective in high-dimensional spaces

Decision Trees

Decision trees are one of the most intuitive classification algorithms. They work by recursively splitting the data into subsets based on feature values, forming a tree-like structure where each internal node represents a decision rule, and each leaf node represents an outcome or class label. Decision trees are popular because they are easy to interpret, but they can be prone to overfitting, especially with small datasets.

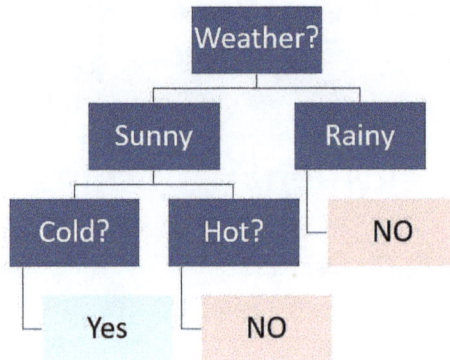

Random Forests

Random forests are an ensemble learning method that combines multiple decision trees to increase classification accuracy and reduce overfitting. Each tree in the forest is trained on a different subset of the data, and the final prediction is made by aggregating the predictions from all trees. This method generally improves robustness and accuracy compared to individual decision trees, making it highly effective for real-world problems.

Random Forests are a powerful ensemble learning method used for making accurate predictions by combining the results of multiple decision trees. To understand how they work, let's consider a simple scenario: predicting whether a person will buy a product based on two features—age (young, middle-aged, or old) and income (low, medium, or high).

The first step in building a Random Forest is to train multiple decision trees on different random subsets of the data. Each tree may use different features or order them differently, which introduces helpful variety into the model.

For instance, tree 1 might use age as the first feature. It could learn that young individuals are less likely to buy the product, while middle-aged people with medium or high income are more likely to make a purchase. In contrast, tree 2 might focus on income as the initial split, concluding that people with high income are likely to buy, and those with low income are not. Tree 3 might combine both features in a different order or follow an entirely different pattern based on its subset of the data.

This variation among trees is intentional—it ensures that each tree captures different aspects of the data, reducing overfitting and improving the overall robustness of the model.

When it comes to making predictions, the process becomes a democratic vote. Suppose we have a new customer who is middle-aged with a medium income. Tree 1 might predict "Yes" based on its age-first rule. Tree 2, focusing more on income, might predict "No." Tree 3, using both features differently, might also predict "Yes."

In the final step, the Random Forest aggregates these individual predictions. Since two of the three trees predict "Yes," the model returns "Yes" as the final prediction. This majority-voting approach helps smooth out errors and leads to more accurate, stable outcomes than a single decision tree would provide.

By combining multiple decision trees, Random Forests create a powerful and flexible model that can handle complexity and variability in real-world data.

Support Vector Machines (SVM)

SVM is a powerful classification algorithm that works by finding the hyperplane that best separates data into distinct classes. The idea is to find the optimal boundary that maximizes the margin between the two classes. SVM is particularly useful in high-dimensional spaces and can be used with both linear and nonlinear data by using kernel functions.

Support Vector Machines (SVMs) are powerful tools used in classification problems, particularly when we want to clearly separate different classes of data. To understand how SVMs work, let's consider a basic scenario where we have two classes of data points—Class A and Class B—plotted on a two-dimensional plane. In this example, the data points are linearly separable, meaning we can draw a straight line to divide the two groups.

The main objective of an SVM is to find the best possible line, or hyperplane, that separates the two classes. But SVM does more than just draw any dividing line. It looks for the one that maximizes the margin—the distance between the line and the closest data points from each class. These closest points are called support vectors. By maximizing the margin, the SVM creates the most robust boundary, reducing the chances of misclassification.

Once the optimal hyperplane is found, the model can be used to classify new data points. If a new point lies on one side of the hyperplane, it is classified as Class A. If it lies on the other side, it is classified as Class B. This decision boundary helps generalize well to unseen data.

However, real-world data is often more complex and not always linearly separable. For instance, if the data points from Class A and Class B are arranged in a circular pattern, a straight line would not suffice. This is where the SVM's flexibility comes into play through the use of the kernel trick. The kernel function allows the SVM to map the original data into a higher-dimensional space where a linear separation is possible. A commonly used kernel is the radial basis function (RBF), which can transform circular or other complex patterns into a form that is linearly separable in the new space.

In summary, SVMs are effective for both simple and complex classification problems. They work by finding the optimal hyperplane that maximizes the margin between classes and can handle non-linear data through kernel functions, making them a versatile choice for many machine learning tasks.

Regression in Data Mining

Regression algorithms are used for predicting continuous numerical values based on input features. Unlike classification, where the output is a category, regression deals with predicting real-valued outcomes. A typical example of regression in action is predicting the price of a house based on factors like location, size, and number of bedrooms.

Linear Regression

Linear regression assumes a linear relationship between the input features and the target variable. It fits a line that best describes the relationship between the independent variables (inputs) and the dependent variable (output). Despite its simplicity, linear regression is widely used due to its efficiency and interpretability.

Ridge and Lasso Regression

These are variations of linear regression that introduce regularization techniques to prevent overfitting. Ridge regression adds a penalty to the magnitude of the coefficients, while Lasso regression also allows for some coefficients to be reduced to zero, effectively performing feature selection. Both methods are valuable when dealing with datasets with many features, where overfitting might be a concern.

Polynomial Regression

Polynomial regression extends linear regression by using polynomial functions to model nonlinear relationships. It allows the algorithm to fit more complex curves to the data, which can improve performance when dealing with data that does not follow a simple linear trend.

133

Logistic Regression

Logistic regression is another important algorithm in regression techniques, although it is primarily used for classification problems. Unlike linear regression, which predicts continuous values, logistic regression predicts the probability that an event occurs, making it ideal for binary outcomes. A common example is predicting whether a customer will purchase a product based on various factors, such as age, income, and previous purchasing behavior. The logistic regression model outputs values between 0 and 1, which can be interpreted as the probability of the event happening. It is widely used in various applications, from medical diagnosis to marketing campaign analysis.

Regression Algorithm	When to Use	Explanation
Linear Regression	Use when the relationship between input features and the target variable is linear.	Linear relationship between inputs (features) and outputs (target). Simple, efficient, interpretable, and widely used for problems like predicting house prices based on square footage, number of rooms, etc.
Ridge Regression	Use when you have a dataset with many features and need to prevent overfitting by introducing regularization.	Regularized version of linear regression. Adds penalty to the model's complexity (magnitude of coefficients), helping to prevent overfitting, especially when features are highly correlated.
Lasso Regression	Use when you have a high-dimensional dataset and want to perform feature selection by reducing some coefficients to zero.	L1 regularization (penalty) that not only prevents overfitting but also eliminates unimportant features by shrinking their coefficients to zero. It's useful for data with many irrelevant features.
Polynomial Regression	Use when the relationship between input features and target is nonlinear, and you need to fit more complex curves.	Extends linear regression to handle nonlinear relationships by adding polynomial terms of the input features. Useful when the data shows a curving trend rather than a straight line.
Logistic Regression	Use when the target variable is binary (e.g., yes/no, true/false, 0/1) and you want to predict the probability of an event occurring.	Classification problem, not traditional regression, but still referred to as "regression" because it models the relationship between independent variables and the probability of an event (output between 0 and 1). Useful in binary classification tasks like predicting customer churn, disease diagnosis, etc.

Clustering Techniques

Clustering is an unsupervised learning technique used to group similar data points together based on shared characteristics, without the need for labeled data. Clustering is particularly useful for exploring data, identifying patterns, and uncovering hidden structures that might not be immediately apparent. Unlike classification, where the classes are predefined, clustering allows the algorithm to discover inherent groupings within the data.

K-Means Clustering

K Means Clustering

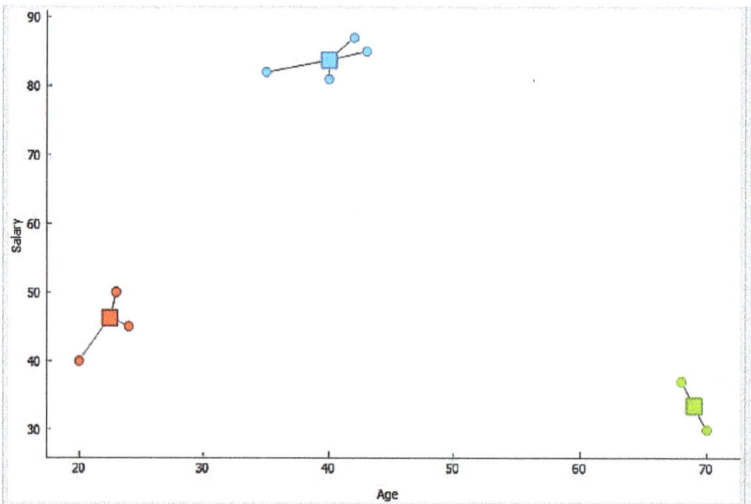

K-means is one of the most widely used clustering algorithms. The goal of K-means is to partition data into 'k' clusters, where each cluster is represented by a central point (the cluster center). The algorithm works by randomly initializing 'k' cluster centers, assigning each data point to the nearest center, and then recalculating the cluster centers based on the mean of the assigned points. This process is repeated iteratively until the cluster assignments no longer change, resulting in stable clusters.

K-means is highly efficient and works well for large datasets. However, it requires the user to specify the number of clusters in advance, which can be a limitation when the optimal number of clusters is unknown.

Hierarchical Clustering

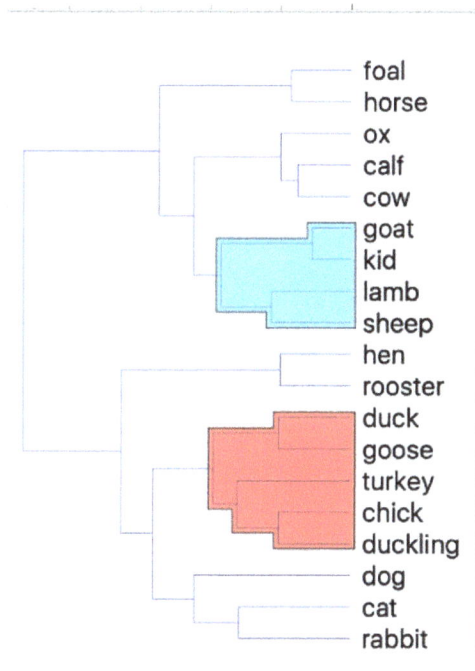

Hierarchical clustering builds a tree-like structure (dendrogram) that represents the nested grouping of data points. This method can be agglomerative (bottom-up), where each data point starts as its own cluster and merges with others iteratively, or divisive (top-down), where all data points begin in a single cluster and are split into smaller clusters. Hierarchical clustering does not require the number of clusters to be specified beforehand, making it more flexible than K-means.

This method is useful for understanding the relationships between clusters and provides a visual representation of how clusters are merged or divided at each step. However, hierarchical clustering can be computationally expensive for large datasets.

DBSCAN

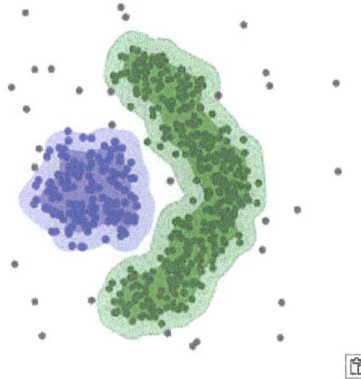

DBSCAN (Density-Based Spatial Clustering of Applications with Noise) is a density-based clustering algorithm that groups data points based on areas of high point density. Unlike K-means, DBSCAN does not require the number of clusters to be specified in advance. Instead, it relies on two parameters: the maximum distance between two points for them to be considered part of the same cluster, and the minimum number of points required to form a dense region (a cluster). DBSCAN is particularly effective at handling noise and outliers in the data, as it can identify points that do not belong to any cluster.

DBSCAN is commonly used in applications such as anomaly detection, spatial data analysis, and geographical data clustering. It is well-suited for identifying clusters with arbitrary shapes and can handle datasets with varying densities.

Review Questions

1. What is the difference between classification and regression?
2. How does a Decision Tree work?
3. What is K-Means clustering?
4. What is the main difference between K-Means and DBSCAN?
5. What does Linear Regression predict?

5-3 Text Data Analysis

Learning Outcomes

5-3-1 Understand what Natural Language Processing (NLP) is.

5-3-2 Describe key NLP tasks.

5-3-3 Use sentiment analysis to understand emotions in text.

5-3-4 Understand topic modeling and how it finds themes in text.

5-3-5 Recognize how NLP is used in real-world applications.

Text data is unstructured, abundant, and often a key source of information in many real-world applications. It is frequently found in sources such as social media posts, customer feedback, news articles, emails, and product reviews. Analyzing and deriving insights from this vast amount of text data requires specialized techniques. Natural Language Processing (NLP) is a critical technology in this area, enabling machines to process and understand human language. NLP combines linguistics, machine learning, and data mining methods to facilitate the analysis of textual content, making it possible to extract meaningful information from vast and varied sources of text.

Basics of Natural Language Processing (NLP)

Natural Language Processing (NLP) is a subfield of artificial intelligence (AI) focused on enabling machines to understand, interpret, and generate human language in a manner that is both meaningful and useful. Through NLP, computers are not just able to process text data but also to extract insights, understand context, and even generate human-like text. NLP is used in a variety of applications, including chatbots, voice assistants, sentiment analysis, machine translation, and much more.

NLP consists of several key tasks, which help break down and interpret text data in ways that computers can process and analyze effectively. Some of the most important NLP tasks include:

Tokenization

Tokenization is the process of breaking down a text into smaller units called "tokens." These tokens are usually words, phrases, or even sentences, and serve as the building blocks for more advanced analysis. Tokenization simplifies raw text into a form that can be processed by algorithms. For example, in a sentence like "I love programming," tokenization would split the text into the individual words "I," "love," and "programming."

Part-of-Speech Tagging

Part-of-speech tagging involves identifying the grammatical components of a sentence, such as nouns, verbs, adjectives, adverbs, and other parts of speech. This task is crucial for understanding the structure and meaning of a sentence. For example, in the sentence "The cat sleeps peacefully," a part-of-speech tagger would identify "cat" as a noun, "sleeps" as a verb, and "peacefully" as an adverb. Part-of-speech tagging allows the computer to understand how words interact with each other, helping in more complex tasks such as sentence parsing and meaning extraction.

Named Entity Recognition (NER)

Named Entity Recognition (NER) refers to the task of detecting and classifying specific entities in text. These entities can include names of people, locations, organizations, dates, and other important concepts. For example, in the sentence "Barack Obama was born in Hawaii on August 4, 1961," an NER system would recognize "Barack Obama" as a person, "Hawaii" as a location, and "August 4, 1961" as a date. NER is important for extracting structured information from unstructured text, which can then be used for further analysis, such as identifying key actors in a news article or categorizing documents.

> **Example**
>
> In natural language processing (NLP), several key tasks are involved in understanding and analyzing text.
>
> For example, given the sentence, "Albert Einstein was born in Ulm, Germany, on March 14, 1879," the first task is tokenization, which breaks the text into smaller units (tokens).
>
> The result of tokenization would be: ["Albert", "Einstein", "was", "born", "in", "Ulm", "Germany", "on", "March", "14", "1879"].
>
> The next task is part-of-speech tagging, where each word is identified by its grammatical role, such as "Albert" being a proper noun, "was" and "born" as verbs, and "Ulm" and "March" as proper nouns. T
>
> he third task, named entity recognition (NER), identifies key entities such as "Albert Einstein" as a person, "Ulm" and "Germany" as locations, and "March 14, 1879" as a date. These tasks—tokenization, part-of-speech tagging, and NER—are essential for machines to process and understand text effectively.

Sentiment Analysis and Topic Modeling

While NLP techniques like tokenization, part-of-speech tagging, and named entity recognition lay the groundwork for text analysis, other more specialized techniques are also employed to derive deeper insights from text data. These include sentiment analysis and topic modeling, both of which help to uncover trends and emotional tones in large volumes of text.

Sentiment Analysis

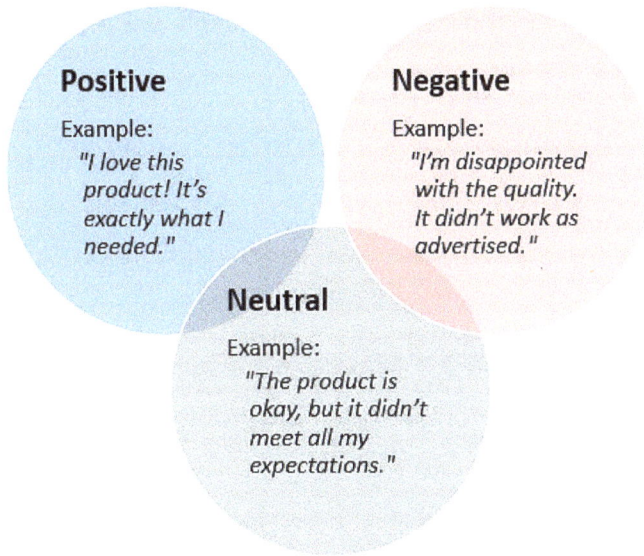

Positive

Example:

"I love this product! It's exactly what I needed."

Negative

Example:

"I'm disappointed with the quality. It didn't work as advertised."

Neutral

Example:

"The product is okay, but it didn't meet all my expectations."

Sentiment analysis is a valuable method for understanding the emotional tone expressed in text. It's commonly used on user-generated content like customer reviews, social media posts, feedback forms, and online comments. The main aim is to categorize the sentiment as positive, negative, or neutral. In customer feedback, sentiment analysis offers organizations important insights into how people feel about their products, services, or experiences.

For example, a review stating, "This phone is amazing! The camera quality is outstanding!" would be labeled as positive, while a comment like "This phone is terrible. The screen cracked after two days" would be tagged negative. By analyzing large amounts of text, sentiment analysis helps companies spot trends in customer satisfaction, identify areas needing improvement, and monitor how their brand is perceived over time.

There are various ways to perform sentiment analysis, ranging from rule-based methods that rely on specific keywords linked to sentiments, to machine learning models trained to classify sentiment from data. More advanced approaches, including deep learning, can even pick up on nuances such as sarcasm or emotions that depend on context.

Example

Sentiment analysis is a method used to determine the overall sentiment in customer reviews, classifying them as positive, negative, or neutral. For instance, in a review where a customer says, "This phone is amazing! The camera quality is outstanding," the sentiment is clearly positive. Words like "amazing" and "outstanding" suggest satisfaction and admiration for the product. In contrast, a review that states, "This phone is terrible. The screen cracked after two days" conveys a negative sentiment. The words "terrible" and "cracked" indicate dissatisfaction and frustration with the product's quality. Lastly, a review like, "The phone works fine, but it's nothing special," is neutral. It neither expresses strong positive nor negative emotions, as the customer is simply indifferent or unimpressed with the product.

Sentiment analysis works by examining emotional cues in the language used within the review to classify the overall tone. This technique allows businesses to gauge customer opinions, identify issues, and improve their products or services based on consumer feedback.

Topic Modeling

Topic modeling is an unsupervised machine learning technique that helps uncover the underlying themes or topics within a large collection of text documents. By analyzing the co-occurrence patterns of words, topic modeling can identify clusters of words that frequently appear together, which are interpreted as topics. One of the most popular methods for topic modeling is Latent Dirichlet Allocation (LDA), which assigns each document in a collection to a set of topics and each word to a topic, based on probability.

For example, in a collection of news articles, LDA might identify topics such as "politics," "sports," and "technology," based on the frequency with which certain words (e.g., "election," "ballgame," "smartphone") appear in each article. Topic modeling helps to organize large text datasets into meaningful clusters, enabling organizations to easily identify the main themes in a body of content.

Topic modeling has applications in many areas, including market research, content recommendation, and trend analysis. For example, a company might use topic modeling to analyze customer feedback and identify common complaints or desires. Similarly, researchers might use topic modeling to analyze academic papers and discover emerging trends in a field.

Example

One effective method for discovering hidden themes in large collections of text is topic modeling, and Latent Dirichlet Allocation (LDA) is a popular technique used for this purpose. LDA allows us to uncover main topics in a collection of documents, which can be invaluable for organizing and analyzing text, such as news articles. To demonstrate how LDA works, we can analyze five news articles from different topics, including politics, sports, and technology, to uncover their main themes.

The first article discusses the upcoming election and voter concerns about healthcare and the economy. The second article covers a football game, emphasizing the excitement surrounding the game and a star player's game-winning touchdown. The third article introduces a new smartphone with cutting-edge features like a high-resolution camera. The fourth article focuses on election debates, where candidates discuss policies related to healthcare and tax reforms. The fifth article looks forward to the basketball championship, with fans eagerly anticipating the final game.

Before applying LDA, we preprocess the articles by removing stop words and tokenizing the text into key terms, such as "election," "football," and "smartphone." Once the articles are processed, LDA identifies three main topics. The first topic is related to politics, with words like "election," "healthcare," and "president" frequently appearing. The second topic is sports, with words such as "football," "game," "player," and "championship" being prominent. The third topic is technology, focusing on terms like "smartphone," "technology," "camera," and "features."

Using the results from LDA, each article is classified according to the topic that best represents its content. Articles discussing the election and political issues are classified under politics, while those about the football game and basketball championship fall under sports. The article about the smartphone is classified under technology. This process allows for automatic grouping of similar content, making it easier to analyze large sets of data, such as news articles, by their main topics.

Review Questions

1. What is NLP and why is it important?
2. What is tokenization in NLP?
3. What is Named Entity Recognition (NER)?
4. How does sentiment analysis help with customer feedback?
5. What is topic modeling and how does it work?

Chapter 6

Data Visualization

6-1 Principles of Data Visualization

Learning Outcomes

6-1-1 Understand how data visualization aides communication.

6-1-2 Identify the appropriate chart type to use.

6-1-3 Choose the right visualization based on data.

6-1-4 Simplify visualizations to ensure clarity.

6-1-5 Use color strategically to enhance visualizations.

6-1-6 Identify accessible visualizations for all audiences.

Effective data visualization is about more than just creating visually appealing charts or graphs; it's about conveying the story behind the data in a clear, accurate, and engaging way. Well-designed visuals not only catch the viewer's eye but also help them quickly understand and interpret complex information.

Choosing the Right Visualization

Effective data visualization is a powerful tool that helps communicate insights clearly and accurately. One of the most important aspects of creating a good visualization is selecting the appropriate chart or graph for the data being presented. The correct choice can simplify complex information, making it easier to understand, while the wrong one can lead to confusion and misinterpretation. This guide outlines how to select the right chart based on the type of data being used and the specific purpose of the visualization, along with some best practices to ensure clarity and effectiveness.

Understanding the Purpose of Data Visualization

The first step in creating a meaningful visualization is to clearly understand the message you want to share. Data visualizations are meant to highlight insights and trends, so it's important to pick a chart type that fits your goal. For example, if you want to compare different groups or categories, a bar chart works well because it makes it easy to see differences in quantity. If you're looking to show how something changes over time, a line graph is usually the best choice, as it clearly illustrates trends across a continuous timeline— like tracking sales, temperature, or stock prices. When the goal is to explore the relationship between two variables, a scatter plot is ideal. Scatter plots reveal patterns like correlations, clusters, or outliers, making them great for visualizing connections between continuous data points, such as height and weight or revenue and marketing spend.

Choosing the right chart for your purpose helps your audience understand the data correctly and draw useful conclusions.

Visualization Goals & Purposes

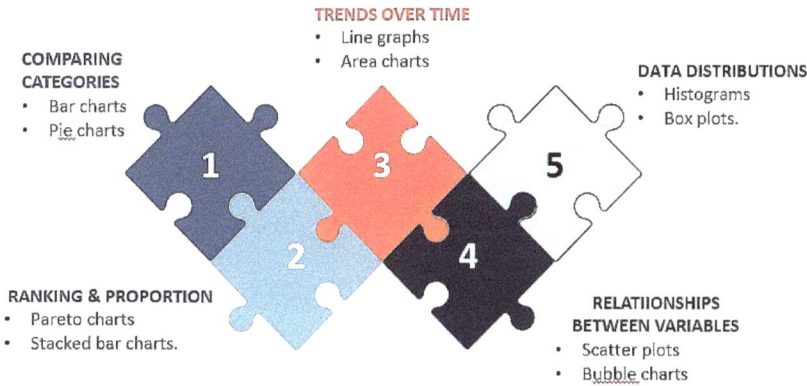

TRENDS OVER TIME
- Line graphs
- Area charts

COMPARING CATEGORIES
- Bar charts
- Pie charts

DATA DISTRIBUTIONS
- Histograms
- Box plots.

1

3

5

2

4

RANKING & PROPORTION
- Pareto charts
- Stacked bar charts.

RELATIIONSHIPS BETWEEN VARIABLES
- Scatter plots
- Bubble charts

Choosing the Right Chart Based on Data Type

Different types of data require different visualization methods to communicate the message clearly. The type of data—whether categorical, time-series, or quantitative—determines which type of chart will be most effective.

When working with categorical data, such as different product types, regions, or demographics, bar charts or pie charts are commonly used. A bar chart can effectively compare the frequency or amount of each category, allowing the viewer to quickly understand how different categories relate to one another. A pie chart, though less commonly used, can also be effective for showing the proportion of each category relative to the whole. For instance, if you want to show how the market share of different companies breaks down, a pie chart can make that proportion visually clear.

For time-series data, which tracks data points over time, line graphs or area charts are typically the best choice. Time-series data may include sales over the course of several months, stock price movements, or changes in temperature over the seasons. Line graphs help the audience observe trends, cycles, and fluctuations, making them particularly useful for showing continuous data over time. Area charts, while similar to line graphs, emphasize the magnitude of change and can help in visualizing the cumulative data over a period.

When analyzing the relationship between two quantitative variables, such as income and education level or height and weight, scatter plots are the most appropriate. Scatter plots display individual data points on a two-dimensional plane, showing how one variable affects another. They are useful for spotting correlations, clusters, or trends that might otherwise be hard to detect. For example, a scatter plot can help identify whether there is a correlation between years of experience and salary for employees within a company.

Best Practices for Data Visualization

While choosing the right chart is crucial, it's also important to follow certain best practices to ensure the visualization is effective and easily interpretable. One of the key principles is simplicity. An effective data visualization should communicate a clear and focused message. Overcomplicating a chart with too many data points or unnecessary elements can confuse the viewer. For example, including too many variables in one chart or using multiple chart types within a single visualization can overwhelm the audience and make it difficult to extract key insights.

To avoid this, it's best to keep the visualization simple and focused on the most important data. This doesn't mean you should omit critical information, but rather that you should prioritize clarity. For instance, if you are showing trends in sales over time, you should avoid cluttering the graph with too many additional data series that could distract from the main insight. Additionally, when presenting time-series data, it's crucial to maintain consistency in the time intervals, so the audience can easily follow the changes over time.

Common Data Visualization Errors

Error	Description	Example
Overcrowding	Too many data points or variables on one graph.	A scatter plot with too many points, making it hard to see trends.
Misleading Scales	Distorting trends with inappropriate scales.	A line graph that starts at a high value, exaggerating trends.
Unclear Labels	Failing to label axes, categories, or legends.	A chart without axis labels, making it unclear what data is shown.

Labels and scales are also essential to ensuring clarity. Always make sure that axis labels, titles, and legends are clear and easy to understand. Avoid using overly technical terms or abbreviations that may confuse the audience. For example, when showing a scatter plot of revenue versus marketing spend, include clear axis labels such as "Revenue (in millions)" and "Marketing Spend (in thousands)" to avoid any ambiguity.

Finally, it's important to remember that visuals should reinforce the message, not obscure it. If a chart is overly complex or filled with extraneous information, it can detract from the core message. The goal is for the audience to walk away with a clear understanding of the data, not to be bogged down by unnecessary details.

By understanding the purpose of your visualization and matching it with the appropriate chart type, you can significantly enhance the clarity of your message. The right chart helps guide the audience to understand key trends, patterns, and relationships in the data. Additionally, simplicity and focus are paramount in ensuring that the visualization remains effective. By following these guidelines, you can create data visualizations that are both informative and engaging, helping your audience make well-informed decisions based on clear, accurate insights.

Certainly! Here's the revised version of the content with fewer sections, written in a more cohesive essay style while still retaining headers:

Color Theory and Design Best Practices

Color is a powerful tool in data visualization, influencing how information is perceived, guiding the viewer's attention, and enhancing the clarity of the visual message. However, color must be used strategically to ensure accessibility, readability, and coherence in the design. Thoughtful application of color theory, considering factors like emotional impact, accessibility, and harmony, can make your visualizations not only aesthetically pleasing but also more effective in conveying key insights.

Understanding Color Psychology and Emotional Impact

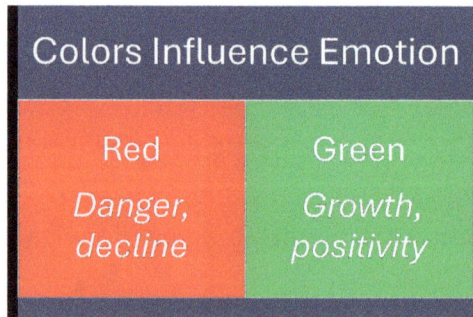

Colors do more than decorate a chart; they can evoke emotions and associations that help reinforce the message being communicated. For instance, red often signals urgency, danger, or a negative trend, while green is commonly associated with growth, positivity, and improvement. By understanding these emotional associations, you can choose colors that align with the message of your visualization. If you're visualizing a decline in sales, using red can instantly convey that negative trend, while green could be used to highlight areas of growth or success.

Strategically applying color can also help draw attention to key data points. For example, using a bright, contrasting color for a particular trend or category can guide the viewer's eye to the most important elements. However, overusing different colors can overwhelm the viewer and make the data harder to interpret. Therefore, it's crucial to use color sparingly, ensuring that it highlights important data without creating unnecessary confusion.

Accessibility and Contrast Considerations

Accessibility is a crucial aspect of color design, especially when considering individuals with color vision deficiencies. A significant portion of the population may have difficulty distinguishing between certain colors, such as red and green, which can impair the understanding of your visualization. Tools like ColorBrewer offer color schemes that are optimized for colorblind accessibility, ensuring that all viewers can easily differentiate between elements in your chart.

In addition to color vision deficiencies, ensuring good contrast between text and background colors is essential for readability. High contrast makes it easier to read the data, especially in low-light conditions or for individuals with visual impairments. For instance, dark text on a light background or light text on a dark background provides the best contrast and improves legibility.

155

Color Harmony and Aesthetic Appeal

While functionality is important, the visual appeal of your chart should not be overlooked. Color harmony refers to the use of colors that work well together to create a visually balanced and pleasing design. Color schemes like complementary (colors on opposite sides of the color wheel, such as blue and orange) or analogous (colors next to each other, like blue, blue-green, and green) can be used to create a cohesive and aesthetically pleasing chart without overwhelming the viewer. When well-executed, color harmony can help maintain the viewer's engagement and support the communication of the data.

For categorical data, it is best to limit the number of colors used to avoid confusion. Too many colors can make it difficult for viewers to differentiate between categories, so a smaller, consistent palette is often more effective. For continuous data, such as temperature or population density, using color gradients allows the viewer to easily interpret the magnitude of values, with darker or lighter shades representing higher or lower values, respectively.

Consistency Across Visualizations

Consistency is key when using color in multiple visualizations. Maintaining a consistent color scheme across a report or dashboard ensures that the viewer can easily follow the data. If a particular color represents a specific category or value in one chart, it should represent the same category in all other related charts. This consistency reduces cognitive load, making it easier for the audience to understand and interpret the data across different visualizations.

By keeping the color palette consistent and applying it thoughtfully throughout your report, you can create a seamless experience for the viewer. This allows them to focus on the data without being distracted or confused by frequent color changes.

Review Questions

1. Why is data visualization important?
2. When should you use a bar chart or a pie chart?
3. What chart works best for showing trends over time?
4. How can you simplify a chart to make it clearer?
5. How does color affect how we see data?
6. How can you make sure your chart works for people with color blindness?

6-2 Graphs

Learning Outcomes

6-2-1 Identify when to use what graph type.
6-2-2 Understand how bar charts are used to compare categories.
6-2-3 Recognize the benefits of line graphs for tracking trends over time.
6-2-4 Interpret how scatter plots reveal relationships.
6-2-5 Understand how histograms display data distribution.
6-2-6 Interpret box plots.

Graphs and charts are essential tools in data visualization, transforming raw data into clear, understandable visuals that help communicate key insights. Choosing the right type of graph or chart is critical for accurately representing data and ensuring that the message is conveyed effectively. Depending on the nature of the data and the analytical goal, different types of graphs serve various purposes. This essay explores the most commonly used types of graphs—bar charts, line graphs, scatter plots, histograms, and box plots—and explains when and how to use each for maximum clarity and impact.

Bar Charts: Ideal for Comparing Categories

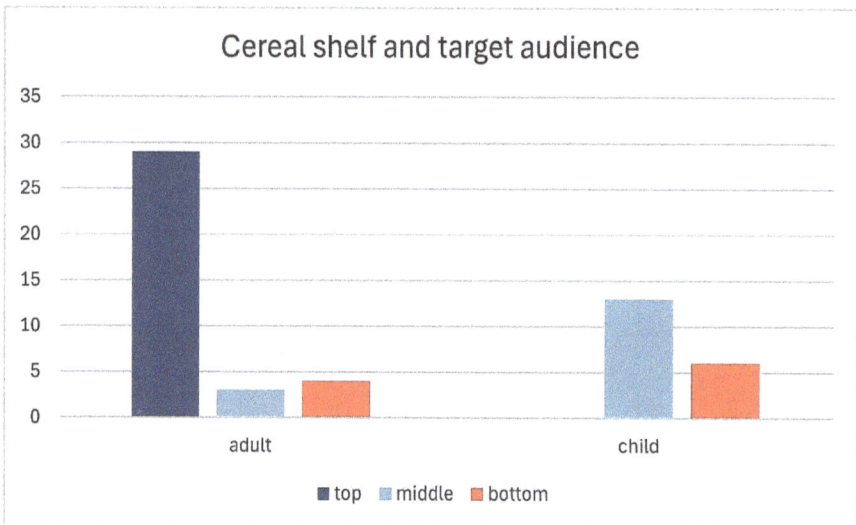

Bar charts are one of the most widely used types of graphs. They are particularly effective when comparing data across different categories. A bar chart displays data with rectangular bars where the length or height of each bar is proportional to the value it represents. This makes bar charts useful for discrete data, such as sales figures across different regions or the number of votes per candidate in an election.

Bar charts can be either vertical or horizontal. Vertical bar charts are often preferred when there are only a few categories to compare, such as sales totals for different products within a specific time period. On the other hand, horizontal bar charts are better suited for situations where category names are long or there are many categories to display. For example, a horizontal bar chart might be used to compare the population of different countries, where the category names (the countries) are lengthy.

Line Graphs: Tracking Trends Over Time

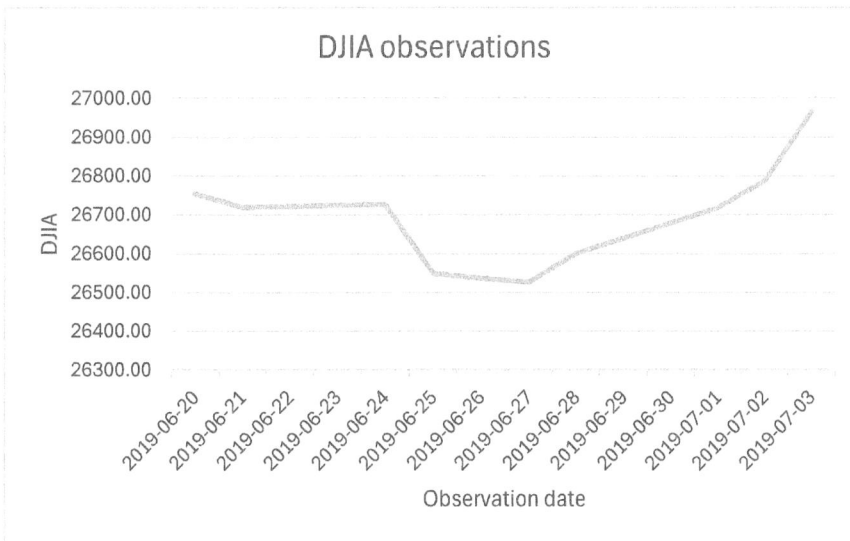

Line graphs are particularly effective when visualizing data that changes over time. They display data points connected by straight lines, making it easy to track changes and identify trends. Line graphs are ideal for continuous data, such as stock prices, temperature variations, or website traffic over several months or years.

The main strength of a line graph lies in its ability to show trends over time. A single line graph can highlight a trend for one dataset, but it can also display multiple lines, allowing for comparisons across different variables or categories. For example, a line graph might be used to compare the sales trends of two competing products over the past year. This makes it clear which product is performing better or whether both are experiencing similar growth patterns.

Scatter Plots: Visualizing Relationships Between Two Variables

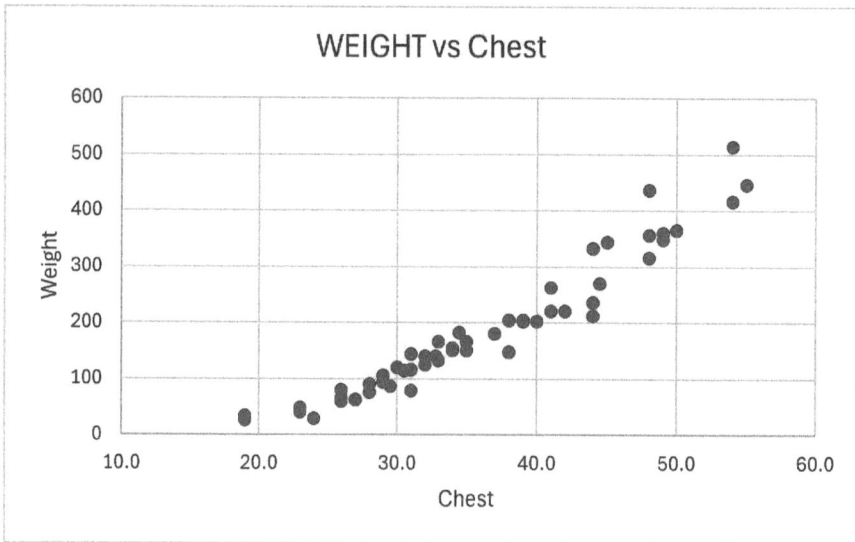

While bar charts and line graphs are used to display data across categories or over time, scatter plots are useful for visualizing the relationship between two continuous variables. A scatter plot displays individual data points on an x and y axis, allowing users to observe correlations, trends, and outliers.

For example, a scatter plot could illustrate the relationship between advertising spending and sales revenue. If there is a positive correlation, the data points will tend to cluster along a diagonal line from the bottom left to the top right. Scatter plots can also reveal if there is no significant relationship between variables or if there are any outliers that deviate from the expected trend. Adding a trend line or a regression line to the scatter plot can further highlight the general direction of the relationship between the two variables.

Histograms: Understanding Data Distribution

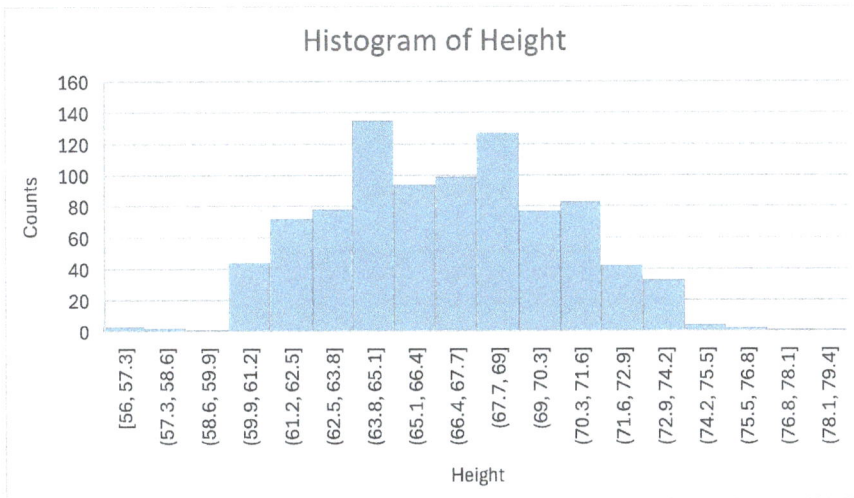

Histograms are a powerful tool for visualizing the distribution of continuous data. A histogram divides the data into intervals or "bins" and displays the frequency of data points within each bin. The height of each bar in the histogram represents how many data points fall into that interval. This helps identify patterns in the data, such as whether values are concentrated in a specific range or if there are any extreme values.

For example, a histogram could be used to visualize the distribution of exam scores in a class. The bins might represent score ranges, such as 50-60%, 60-70%, and so on. By looking at the histogram, one could easily see whether most students scored in the 60-70% range or if the scores were more evenly spread out across the entire range.

Box Plots: Summarizing Data Spread

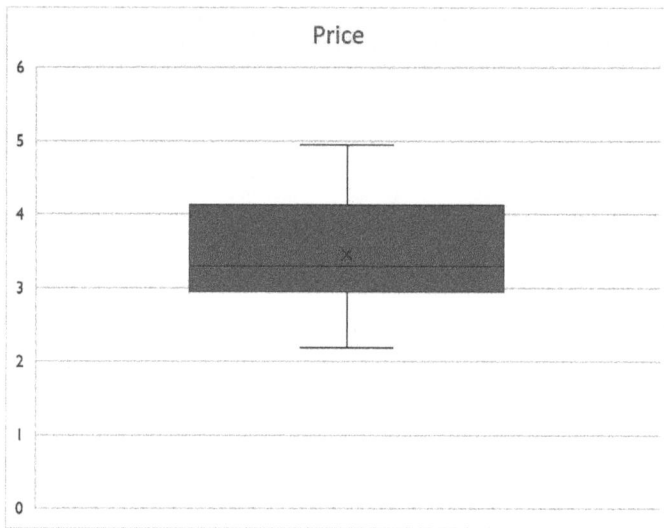

Box plots, also known as box-and-whisker plots, provide a summary of a dataset's distribution. A box plot displays the median, quartiles, and potential outliers within the data. The "box" represents the interquartile range (the range between the first and third quartiles), and the "whiskers" show the range of values within 1.5 times the interquartile range.

Box plots are particularly helpful when comparing the distribution of data across multiple categories or datasets. For instance, a box plot could be used to compare the exam scores of students in different courses or the salary distribution across different job titles. The box plot shows not only the median and spread of the data but also highlights potential outliers, which could indicate unusual data points that may require further investigation.

Review Questions

1. When should you use a bar chart instead of a line graph?
2. What type of data is best represented by a scatter plot?
3. How does a line graph help in understanding trends over time?
4. What does a histogram show about the distribution of data?
5. What is the purpose of a box plot in data visualization?
6. How do you determine when to use a horizontal bar chart over a vertical one?
7. What is the benefit of adding a trend line to a scatter plot?

6-3 Geographic Data and Mapping

Learning Outcomes

6-3-1 Understand the different types of geographic data and their applications.

6-3-2 Identify key tools for geographic data visualization.

6-3-3 Evaluate different types of maps for visualizing spatial data.

6-3-4 Apply geographic data analysis to real-world scenarios.

6-3-5 Recognize the importance of interactivity in maps.

Geographic data has become an essential tool in various industries, offering valuable insights into patterns, distributions, and trends that are tied to specific locations. With the advancement of technology, industries such as marketing, urban planning, and public health increasingly rely on geographic data to inform decision-making. These tools help to visualize data in a spatial context, enabling organizations to make more informed, location-based decisions.

Types of Geographic Data and Their Applications

Geographic data can be classified into three primary types: point data, area data, and raster data. Each type serves a distinct purpose, allowing for different applications in various sectors.

Point Data refers to specific locations represented by coordinates (latitude and longitude). This type of data is ideal for pinpointing exact locations such as stores or landmarks. For example, businesses often use point data to identify areas with high concentrations of customers or to evaluate the locations of competitor stores.

Area Data encompasses larger geographical regions like cities, neighborhoods, or countries. It is useful for analyzing broader trends such as population density or regional income distribution. Urban planners and businesses use area data to make decisions about resource allocation, infrastructure development, and market opportunities.

Raster Data involves continuous data across a grid, with each cell containing a value such as temperature, air quality, or elevation. Raster data is particularly valuable in environmental monitoring and helps visualize factors that change over large geographic areas, such as climate patterns or deforestation.

These types of geographic data are crucial in several applications, such as market analysis, urban planning, and public health. Businesses use spatial data to assess customer distribution and identify new market opportunities. City planners leverage geographic data to design transportation systems, manage urban growth, and address environmental issues. Additionally, health departments use geospatial data to track disease outbreaks and allocate medical resources effectively.

Creating Maps for Analysis

Maps are one of the most effective ways to visualize geographic data. They help to simplify complex datasets and allow users to detect patterns and trends within a spatial context. Various types of maps are employed to display and analyze geographic information.

Geographic Maps

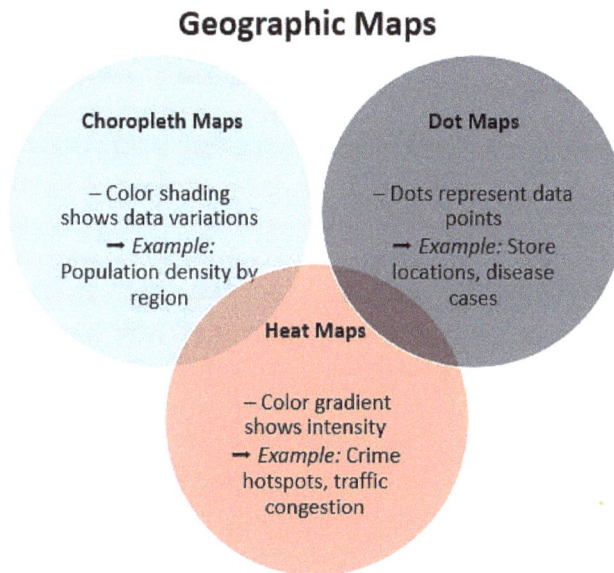

Choropleth Maps
— Color shading shows data variations
→ *Example:* Population density by region

Dot Maps
— Dots represent data points
→ *Example:* Store locations, disease cases

Heat Maps
— Color gradient shows intensity
→ *Example:* Crime hotspots, traffic congestion

Choropleth Maps are used to visualize the variation of a variable across different geographic regions. By applying color shading, these maps indicate differences in values such as population density or income. Darker areas often represent higher values, making it easier to identify regions with significant demographic or economic characteristics.

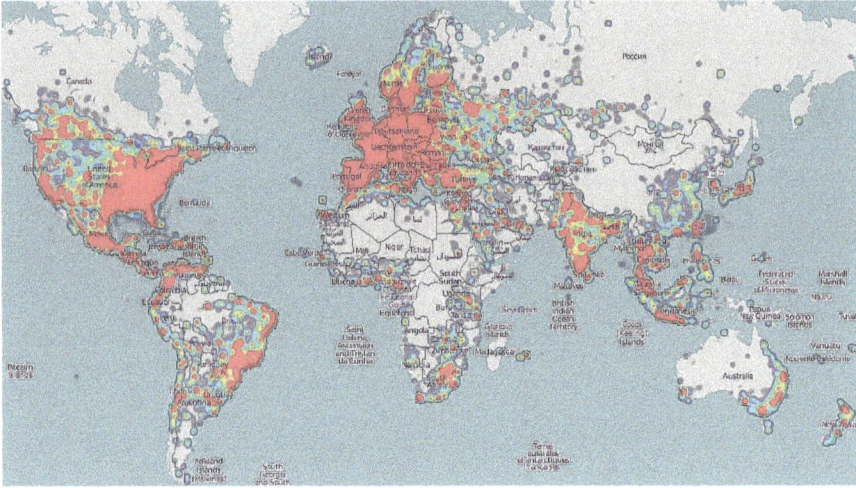

Heat Maps use color gradients to represent the intensity of a variable. For example, a heat map might display crime rates, with red areas indicating high crime frequency and cooler colors showing lower crime levels. Heat maps are particularly useful for highlighting areas with concentrated activity or issues.

Dot Maps display data using dots to represent individual data points, with the density of dots indicating the concentration of a variable. For example, a dot map might be used to show the location of stores or facilities, where a higher concentration of dots indicates a greater number of establishments in that region.

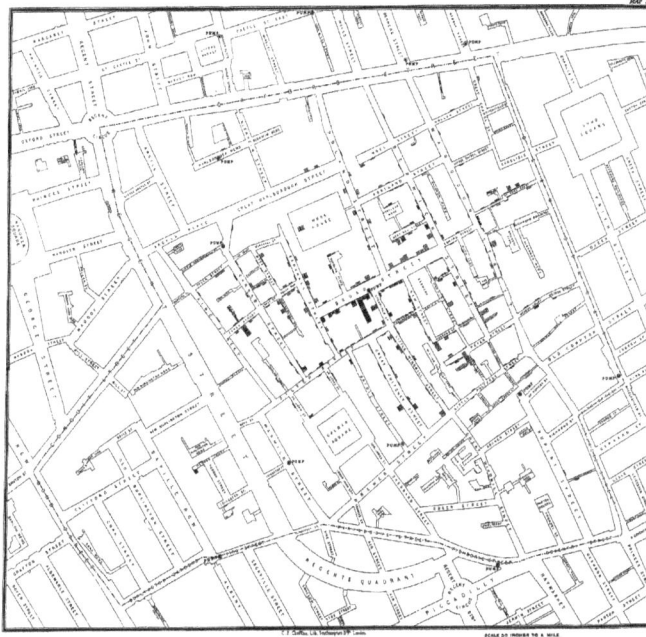

Tools for Geographic Data Visualization

To effectively create and analyze geographic data, specialized tools are required. Geographic Information Systems (GIS) and other mapping platforms offer powerful solutions for visualization and spatial analysis.

GIS Tools, such as ArcGIS and QGIS, are advanced software used to layer multiple types of geographic data and perform detailed spatial analysis. These tools allow users to create sophisticated maps, identify patterns, and conduct geographic studies. GIS tools are commonly used in urban planning, environmental research, and disaster management.

Mapping Platforms, like Google Maps, Tableau, and Mapbox, provide user-friendly alternatives for geographic data visualization. These platforms allow users to create interactive maps and visualize geographic information without requiring deep technical knowledge. For instance, users can overlay custom data layers on Google Maps or create visually appealing maps with Tableau, making these tools accessible for a wide range of users.

Interactivity in Maps

Interactive maps offer dynamic functionality that allows users to engage with the data more effectively. Users can zoom in on areas, filter data, or click on elements to access more detailed information. For example, an interactive map may allow a user to view detailed traffic patterns for a specific region or filter population data by age group or income level. The ability to interact with maps enhances the user experience, providing deeper insights by enabling exploration of the data in a personalized and meaningful way. These features are particularly useful for decision-making processes that require more granular analysis or a focus on specific geographic areas.

Review Questions

1. What are the three main types of geographic data?
2. How is point data different from area data and raster data?
3. How can geographic data help businesses and urban planners make decisions?
4. What is a choropleth map, and when would it be used?
5. How does a heat map represent geographic data, and what does it show?
6. How is a dot map used to represent geographic data?
7. What role does GIS play in geographic data analysis?
8. Why is interactivity important in geographic maps?

6-4 Storytelling with Data

Learning Outcomes

6-4-1 Identify Key Principles of Effective Data Visualization.

6-4-2 Utilize Contextualization in Visualizations.

6-4-3 Highlight Key Insights in Data Visualizations.

6-4-4 Differentiate Between Dashboards and Reports.

6-4-5 Select Appropriate Tools for Data Visualization storytelling.

Data visualization is far more than just the creation of charts or graphs; it serves as a bridge between complex datasets and actionable insights. The goal is to turn raw data into a narrative that makes it both understandable and meaningful. When done well, data visualization doesn't just present facts—it tells a story that helps people make informed decisions. Below, we explore how effective data visualization communicates insights clearly, simplifies complex data, and utilizes dashboards and reports to drive meaningful action.

Effective Data Visualization

In today's data-driven world, the ability to communicate insights clearly and efficiently is just as important as the data itself. Effective data visualization bridges the gap between complex datasets and actionable understanding by transforming raw numbers into visual stories that inform decision-making. It is not enough for a visualization to look appealing—it must also be purposeful, contextual, and focused on the message it aims to deliver. When done well, data visualization helps audiences quickly grasp key insights, identify trends, and draw meaningful conclusions, making it an essential skill for anyone working with data.

Communicating Insights Clearly

The primary goal of data visualization is to communicate insights clearly and effectively. If the visualization lacks clarity, even the most well-crafted data presentation can be misinterpreted or overlooked. A well-designed visualization should convey the intended message without confusion, making it easier for the audience to understand and act upon the information.

Contextualizing the Data

One of the key elements of effective data visualization is providing context. Data without context can be misleading or confusing. It's essential to explain what the data represents and why it matters. For example, if a sales graph shows a sudden decline, it is crucial to include context, such as market conditions or competitor actions, to help the audience understand the reasons behind the drop. Annotations or explanatory text within the visual can be useful tools to highlight important trends, outliers, or anomalies, ensuring that viewers grasp the full picture.

Highlighting Key Insights

Data visualization should not simply display numbers—it should highlight the key insights within the data. By emphasizing significant trends or changes, viewers can quickly focus on the most important points. This can be achieved through visual elements such as bold colors, arrows, or callouts. For instance, a graph tracking sales might use a bright color to highlight a spike in performance during a specific period, making it easier for the viewer to spot this significant change and understand its relevance.

Simplifying Complex Data

Large datasets can often overwhelm viewers, making it difficult to extract meaningful insights. To address this, data should be broken down into simpler, more digestible visual representations. By focusing on the essential data points and presenting them in a way that is easy to understand at a glance, you can make complex information more accessible. For example, summarizing trends or aggregating data into high-level insights can allow the audience to quickly grasp the most important information without being bogged down by unnecessary details.

Communicating insights through data visualization requires careful consideration of context, the highlighting of key insights, and simplifying complex information. When these elements are applied effectively, a data visualization becomes a powerful tool for delivering clear, actionable insights to the audience.

Example

Quarterly Sales Performance Summary

A line graph presents sales figures for the past three quarters, with time on the x-axis and sales revenue on the y-axis.

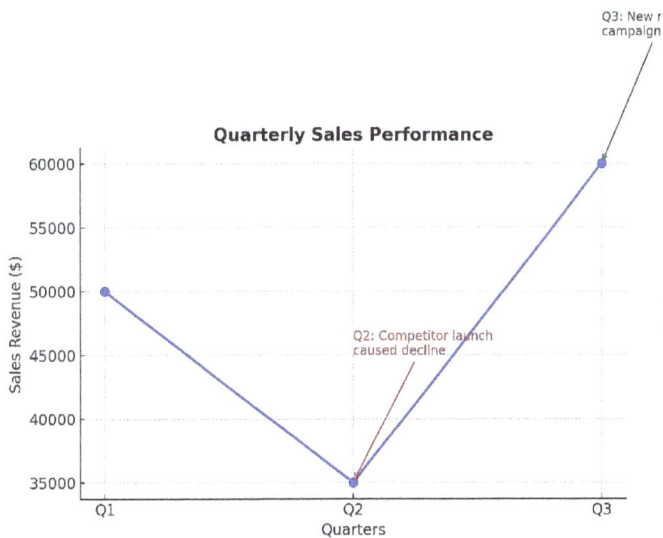

Key Elements

A smooth trend line with clear axis labels and annotations for context. Q2 Sales Decline An annotation explains the drop due to a competitor's product launch. Additional context highlights market downturn effects. Q3 Sales Recovery A noticeable spike in Q3 is highlighted, attributed to a successful marketing strategy.   Simplification for Clarity The focus is on overall quarterly sales trends rather than individual product lines. A trend line is added to show long-term growth

Designing Dashboards and Reports

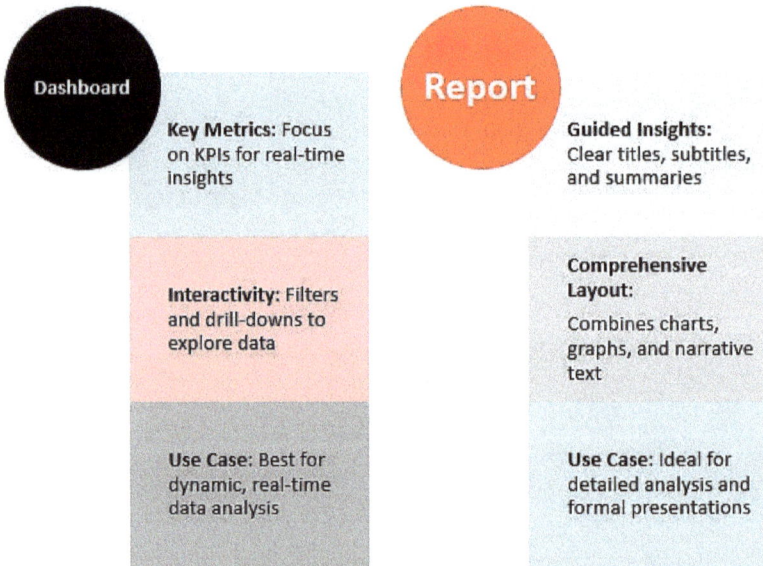

Dashboard

Key Metrics: Focus on KPIs for real-time insights

Interactivity: Filters and drill-downs to explore data

Use Case: Best for dynamic, real-time data analysis

Report

Guided Insights: Clear titles, subtitles, and summaries

Comprehensive Layout: Combines charts, graphs, and narrative text

Use Case: Ideal for detailed analysis and formal presentations

Dashboards and reports are crucial tools for presenting data and insights. Both serve different purposes but share the goal of helping the audience interact with and understand data.

Dashboards and Reports

Dashboards are designed to track real-time data and key performance indicators (KPIs). Their main goal is to present important information clearly and concisely, enabling users to make quick decisions. Key metrics should be prioritized to align with the user's objectives, focusing on the most critical KPIs that drive action. Interactive elements, like filters or drilldowns, allow users to explore data in more detail. For instance, a sales dashboard might allow filtering by region or time period to zoom in on specific data points.

Reports, on the other hand, provide more detailed, narrative-driven insights. They offer an in-depth analysis by integrating various visualizations into a cohesive story. Reports should include guided insights, with clear titles, subtitles, and summaries to help the audience understand the data's significance. Unlike dashboards, reports combine charts, graphs, and text, providing a comprehensive view that often includes recommendations and context to aid in decision-making.

Tools for Creating Dashboards and Reports

In today's data-driven world, presenting data in an accessible and actionable format is crucial for decision-making. Whether the goal is to create an interactive dashboard that allows for real-time analysis or a static report that summarizes key insights, choosing the right tool can significantly impact how easily the data is understood and acted upon. The tools available for both interactive dashboards and static reports vary in features and functionality, making it essential to select the appropriate platform for each specific need.

Interactive Dashboard Tools

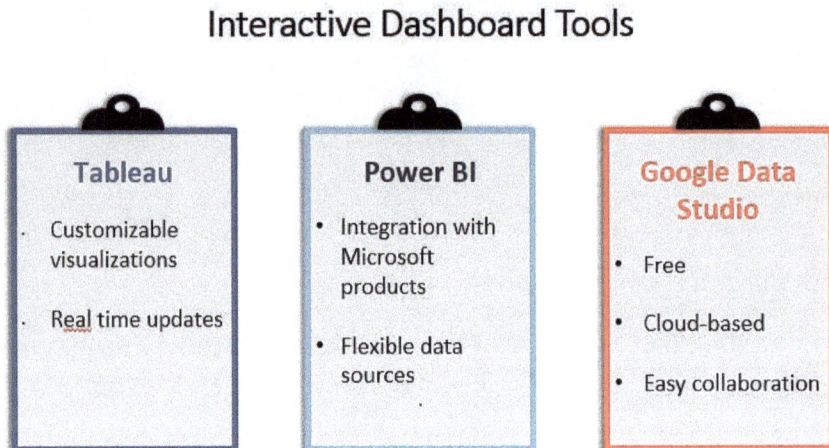

Interactive Dashboard Tools

Tableau
- Customizable visualizations
- Real time updates

Power BI
- Integration with Microsoft products
- Flexible data sources

Google Data Studio
- Free
- Cloud-based
- Easy collaboration

Interactive dashboards are an essential tool for businesses and organizations that need to visualize large volumes of data in a way that enables real-time decision-making. These dashboards allow users to interact with the data, drill down into specific subsets, and customize their views to extract the most relevant information. Several widely used tools are designed specifically for creating interactive dashboards:

Tableau   Tableau is one of the most popular tools for creating interactive dashboards, offering robust capabilities for data visualization. It allows users to connect to various data sources, such as spreadsheets, databases, and cloud services, and creates visually appealing and intuitive dashboards. Tableau's drag-and-drop interface makes it easy to design dashboards that display real-time data insights. Users can customize visualizations and apply filters to drill deeper into the data, making it highly versatile for different business needs.

Power BI   Power BI, developed by Microsoft, is another widely adopted tool for creating interactive dashboards. It integrates seamlessly with other Microsoft products like Excel and Azure, allowing users to easily pull in data from various sources. Power BI offers a wide range of visualizations and customization options, enabling users to create tailored dashboards that fit their specific requirements. Additionally, Power BI provides real-time updates, ensuring that dashboards always reflect the most current data. Its user-friendly interface and integration with familiar tools like Excel make it an excellent choice for users with varying levels of expertise.

Google Data Studio   Google Data Studio is a free, cloud-based tool that enables users to create interactive dashboards and reports. It integrates well with other Google services, such as Google Analytics, Google Sheets, and BigQuery, making it a natural choice for businesses already using Google's ecosystem. Google Data Studio allows users to design custom dashboards that are easy to share and collaborate on in real time. The tool's simplicity and ease of use make it a popular choice for individuals and organizations looking for an accessible platform for creating interactive visualizations.

These interactive dashboard tools offer flexibility in data integration, customization of visuals, and real-time updates, making them ideal for scenarios that require dynamic data exploration and visualization.

Static Report Tools

Static Report Tools

Excel
. Data analysis and simple reporting

Google Sheets
. Collaborative, cloud-based reporting

Adobe InDesign
. Professional, high-quality report design

While interactive dashboards are perfect for real-time data exploration, static reports serve a different purpose. Static reports are designed to summarize and communicate key insights in a fixed format, typically combining data visualizations with text and other graphics. These reports are used for formal presentations, annual reviews, or any situation where a detailed, yet non-interactive, report is needed. Several tools are commonly used for creating static reports:

Excel Excel is one of the most widely used tools for creating static reports, especially when it comes to data analysis and charting. While it may not have the advanced visualization capabilities of tools like Tableau, Excel allows users to perform complex calculations and create various types of charts and graphs. It is particularly useful when the report involves data manipulation or requires a more analytical approach. Excel's ability to generate simple, yet powerful, static reports make it an indispensable tool in business analytics.

Google Sheets   Google Sheets, similar to Excel, offers the ability to create static reports with the added benefit of cloud-based collaboration. Multiple users can work on the same document simultaneously, making it an ideal choice for teams that need to work together on a report. Google Sheets offers many of the same features as Excel, including data manipulation, charting, and analysis, though it may not be as feature-rich in terms of advanced reporting capabilities.

Adobe InDesign   For more polished and professional reports, Adobe InDesign is a leading tool. Unlike Excel or Google Sheets, which are primarily data analysis tools, InDesign is designed for high-quality print and digital publications. It allows users to combine data visualizations with text, graphics, and other design elements, resulting in aesthetically pleasing and highly customizable reports. Adobe InDesign is ideal for creating formal reports, marketing materials, annual reports, and other publications that require a professional layout and design.

Choosing the Right Tool

The choice of tool for creating interactive dashboards or static reports depends largely on the type of data being presented and the level of interactivity required. For dynamic, real-time data exploration, interactive dashboard tools like Tableau, Power BI, and Google Data Studio are the best options. These tools offer flexible, user-friendly interfaces that allow users to integrate data from multiple sources and design visualizations that provide real-time insights, enabling users to interact with and explore the data in depth.

On the other hand, static reports require tools that focus on summarizing data in a fixed format. Excel and Google Sheets are excellent choices for users who need to conduct data analysis and create basic reports. For reports that require a more polished and professional design, Adobe InDesign is the go-to tool, allowing users to create visually appealing reports that combine data visualizations with text and graphics.

Ultimately, the right tool will depend on the specific needs of the user, the type of data being presented, and the desired level of interactivity. By carefully considering these factors, users can choose the tool that best fits their goals and ensures that the data is presented clearly and effectively.

Review Questions

1. Summarize the key principles of effective data visualization
2. What is the difference between dashboards and reports?
3. What features should an interactive dashboard have?
4. What tools can you use to create interactive dashboards?
5. Which tools are best for creating static reports and why?
6. How do you decide which tool to use for dashboards or reports?
7. What design principles should you follow when creating a dashboard?
8. When is it better to use a static report instead of an interactive dashboard?

Chapter 7

AI in Data Analytics

7-1 AI in Data Processing

Data processing is the series of steps involved in collecting, transforming, and organizing raw data into a more usable format for analysis or decision-making. It involves cleaning, sorting, structuring, and sometimes enriching the data to ensure its accurate and useful for further tasks, such as reporting, modeling, or analytics.

Learning Outcomes

7-1-1 Explain the role of AI in automating data processing.
7-1-2 Identify the benefits of AI-powered data processing.
7-1-3 Describe common AI applications in data processing.
7-1-4 Recognize the challenges and limitations of AI-driven automation.

AI in Automating Data Processing

Artificial Intelligence (AI) has transformed how computers process, analyze, and extract insights from large amounts of data with little human involvement. In data analytics, AI is essential for using algorithms, machine learning models, and automation to boost efficiency, increase accuracy, and produce predictive insights. By automating routine and time-consuming tasks, AI frees analysts to concentrate on strategic decisions and complex problem-solving. The influence of AI-powered data processing is felt across many industries.

Benefits of AI in Automated Data Processing

One of the most significant advantages of AI-driven automation is the dramatic increase in processing speed and efficiency. Traditional data processing methods often require extensive manual effort, which can be slow, error-prone, and subject to bottlenecks. AI-powered algorithms can analyze massive datasets in seconds, drastically reducing the time required for essential data operations such as extraction, cleaning, and transformation. This increased speed not only accelerates decision-making but also allows businesses to react more quickly to emerging trends and patterns.

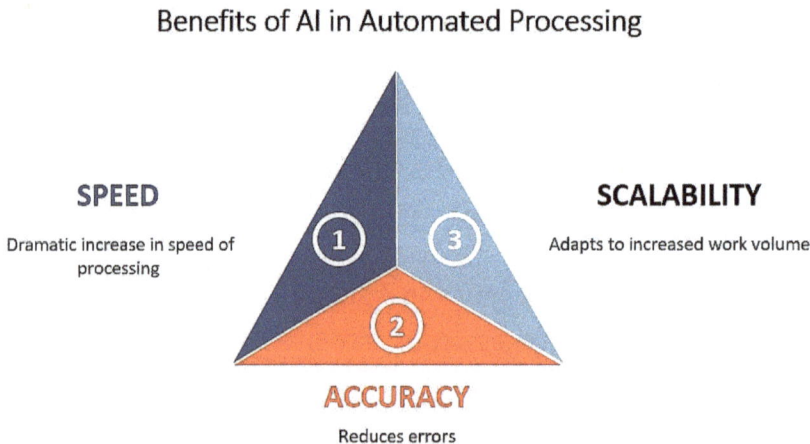

Benefits of AI in Automated Processing

SPEED

Dramatic increase in speed of processing

SCALABILITY

Adapts to increased work volume

ACCURACY

Reduces errors

Beyond improving speed, AI also helps reduce human errors in data handling. Manual processing often leads to mistakes like incorrect entries, duplicate records, and inconsistent formatting. AI-driven automation cuts down these errors by applying standardized workflows and validation checks, which boost accuracy and reliability in data analysis. Still, AI isn't perfect—while it can catch and fix human mistakes, human oversight is needed to make sure AI systems are working properly and adapting to changing data requirements.

Another major benefit of AI in data processing is scalability. As data volumes grow rapidly across industries, traditional manual methods can't keep up with the increasing size, variety, and speed of information. AI-powered systems can efficiently process large and complex datasets, making them highly scalable. This is especially important in fields that generate a lot of unstructured data, like social media, e-commerce, and healthcare. However, it's worth noting that non-AI software has also improved in handling big data, so AI's advantages are most pronounced when working with dynamic or unstructured data sources.

Common Applications of AI in Data Processing

AI-driven automation plays a crucial role in various aspects of data processing.

AI Applications in Data Processing

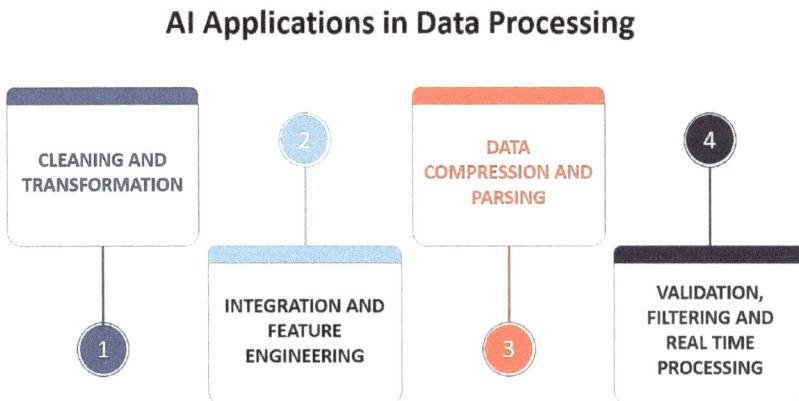

CLEANING AND TRANSFORMATION

2

DATA COMPRESSION AND PARSING

4

1

INTEGRATION AND FEATURE ENGINEERING

3

VALIDATION, FILTERING AND REAL TIME PROCESSING

Data Cleaning and Transformation   AI plays a critical role in automating data cleaning, helping to identify and correct issues such as missing values, duplicates, or errors. It also automates the transformation of data into usable formats, like scaling numerical values or encoding categorical data. This ensures that raw data is in the best shape for further processing or analysis.

Data Integration and Feature Engineering   AI is also used to integrate data from different sources, resolving conflicts and ensuring a consistent structure across datasets. In feature engineering, AI can automatically extract meaningful features from raw data, such as text or images, and reduce irrelevant information, simplifying the data for future use in machine learning models.

Data Compression and Parsing   AI helps in compressing large datasets, making them more manageable without losing important information. Additionally, AI-powered parsing tools can extract relevant details from unstructured data (like text or scanned documents), converting them into structured formats that are easier to work with.

Data Validation, Filtering, and Real-Time Processing   AI can automatically validate data, ensuring its accuracy and integrity before further processing. It also filters out irrelevant or redundant data, reducing the overall data volume. Furthermore, AI is capable of real-time processing, which is essential for analyzing data as it's generated, such as in sensor or streaming applications.

Challenges and Limitations

Despite its many advantages, AI-driven automation in data processing is not without challenges. The reliability of AI models heavily depends on the quality of the data they process. Incomplete, inconsistent, or biased data can lead to inaccurate predictions and flawed insights. This issue underscores the importance of maintaining high-quality data inputs and continuously refining AI models to ensure accuracy.

Additionally, AI should be viewed as an augmentation tool rather than a complete replacement for human analysts. While AI can handle intelligent automated tasks, human oversight remains critical.

AI Automation Balances with Human Oversight

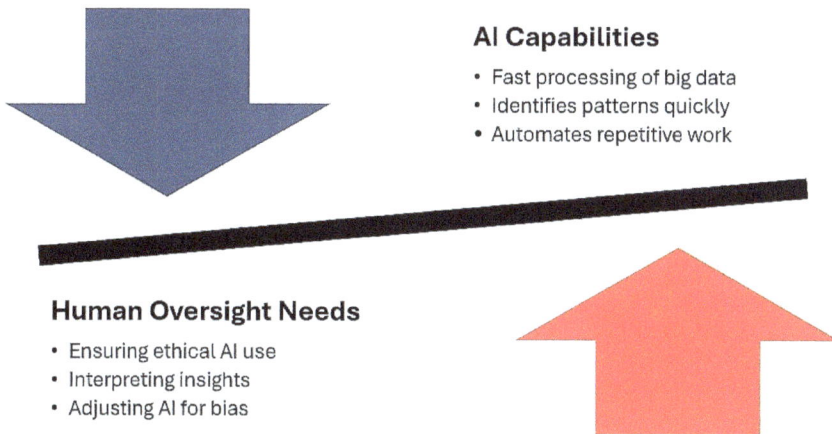

AI Capabilities
- Fast processing of big data
- Identifies patterns quickly
- Automates repetitive work

Human Oversight Needs
- Ensuring ethical AI use
- Interpreting insights
- Adjusting AI for bias

There is also a risk of over-reliance on AI. Blindly trusting AI-generated insights without validation can lead to flawed decision-making. Businesses and organizations must complement AI-driven analysis with human expertise and critical thinking to mitigate potential risks. AI should serve as a powerful tool for enhancing decision-making rather than a substitute for careful analysis and judgment.

Review Questions

1. How does AI contribute to automating data processing?
2. What are some key benefits of AI-powered data processing?
3. Describe three common applications of AI in data processing and explain how they improve efficiency.
4. Why is human oversight necessary when using AI for data processing?

7-2 Insights with AI

AI-driven data discovery is not just about speeding up analysis—it's about uncovering deeper, more meaningful insights that lead to better outcomes. From recognizing patterns and correlations to flagging anomalies and exposing hidden truths, AI has become an indispensable tool in turning data into knowledge.

Learning Outcomes

7-2-1 Explain the role of AI in finding patterns in large sets of data.

7-2-2 Describe how AI can discover relationships (correlations).

7-2-3 Understand how AI helps find unusual or unexpected data (anomalies).

7-2-4 Give examples of how AI finds hidden insights that people might not notice.

7-2-5 Recognize the limits of AI and the need for human oversight.

As organizations collect more data than ever before, the challenge has shifted from gathering data to understanding it. This is where Artificial Intelligence (AI) plays a transformative role. AI helps uncover meaning within vast amounts of information, making it possible to recognize patterns, detect correlations, identify anomalies, and reveal hidden insights with speed and precision. By automating these processes, AI enables businesses and researchers to extract value that would be nearly impossible to find manually.

Analytical Task AI Excels At

PATTERN RECOGNITION

IDENTIFY ANOMALIES

REVEAL HIDDEN INSIGHTS

DETECTING CORRELATIONS

Rapid Pattern Recognition

One of AI's greatest strengths is its ability to quickly spot patterns and trends in massive amounts of data. As datasets grow larger and more complex, it becomes challenging for humans or traditional tools to keep up. Manual analysis can be slow and error-prone, while standard statistical methods may struggle to scale or adjust to evolving patterns.

AI transforms this by automating pattern detection through advanced machine learning algorithms. These algorithms can analyze thousands—or even millions—of data points rapidly, uncovering recurring behaviors, trends, and signals in real time. Unlike fixed models, AI systems learn from historical data and improve their accuracy over time. This adaptability makes them especially valuable in fast-changing environments where conditions and behaviors are always shifting.

Moreover, AI goes beyond detecting obvious patterns—it can reveal subtle or complex trends that human analysts might overlook. It can identify seasonal variations, shifts in behavior, and time-sensitive spikes that are crucial for making decisions. Thanks to its speed and scale, AI enables organizations to react more quickly and effectively.

Example

Detecting Seasonal Demand for Outerwear at NovaWear

NovaWear had long relied on district managers to place seasonal orders based on past experience and manual spreadsheets. This approach led to some stores running out of winter coats before December, while others faced unsold inventory by January. Marketing campaigns often launched too late and failed to account for regional timing differences, such as colder states needing stock earlier.

In 2022, NovaWear implemented TrendSight AI, a cloud-based retail analytics platform. This platform used machine learning to analyze five years of point-of-sale data, local weather patterns, promotional calendars, and web search trends.

The AI identified several key patterns. In northern states like Minnesota and Michigan, coat sales consistently began rising in Week 42 (mid-to-late October) and peaked in Week 47 (late November). In southern states such as Texas and Georgia, coat sales spiked in Weeks 46–48 but on a smaller scale. Additionally, the AI found that accessories like scarves and gloves spiked in the weeks following coat purchases, particularly when bundled in-store or promoted online. As a result, NovaWear took several actions. They staggered inventory shipments based on regional patterns, with northern stores receiving stock earlier. Targeted local ads for coats were launched two weeks before the anticipated sales spike in each region. A new "Winter Ready Bundle" promotion, which included coats and accessories, was also introduced to capitalize on the accessory sales trend.

The impact was significant. Coat sales increased by 15previous year, while excess inventory in southern stores dropped by 21Customers redeemed 42ads, and store managers reported fewer complaints about

out-of-stock items.

Correlation Detection with AI

AI tools are highly skilled at spotting correlations within large datasets. A correlation means that when one factor changes, another tends to change as well. Because AI can quickly process huge amounts of data, it can find these connections much faster than traditional approaches like manual analysis or simple statistical models, which often struggle with big, complex data. By uncovering these relationships, AI helps businesses discover patterns they might otherwise miss.

One major strength of AI in this area is its ability to analyze thousands or even millions of data points at once. Using machine learning algorithms, AI can scan data in real time to detect repeating patterns or links between variables. This makes AI especially useful in fast-paced fields like e-commerce or finance. For example, an AI system might find a strong correlation between how often customers use a mobile app and how much they spend, indicating that more engaged users tend to make bigger purchases.

AI also shines at finding complex correlations that involve multiple variables at the same time. While traditional methods often look at only two variables together, AI can consider many factors simultaneously, revealing subtle relationships that aren't obvious at first glance. For instance, a coffee shop chain might use AI to detect a link between weather conditions, customer demographics, and sales—discovering that hot drink sales rise during rainy days, but mainly among customers aged 30 to 45. This kind of analysis would be very hard for people to do manually.

Another benefit of AI is that it can continuously learn and improve its detection of correlations as new data comes in. Unlike fixed analysis methods, AI systems adapt over time, refining their accuracy based on fresh information. This ongoing learning helps businesses keep their insights current and adjust strategies when needed. For example, a financial institution could use AI to analyze transaction records, customer age, and location to find correlations that inform marketing or product decisions, with these insights becoming sharper as more data is processed.

Identifying Anomalies

AI is particularly effective at detecting anomalies—data points or patterns that significantly deviate from what is considered normal. These outliers may indicate errors, fraud, or rare but critical events. Anomaly detection helps businesses and organizations spot irregularities that could otherwise go unnoticed, allowing for swift action to address potential issues.

AI-powered anomaly detection systems use machine learning algorithms and statistical models to establish a baseline for normal behavior within a dataset. Once this baseline is set, the system can automatically flag data points that diverge sharply from the established norm, alerting users to investigate further. These systems improve over time, learning from new data and becoming more accurate at identifying irregularities.

> **Example**
>
> One common application of AI in anomaly detection is fraud detection in banking. AI tools constantly monitor financial transactions and identify unusual activity, such as a large withdrawal from a foreign country that may indicate a compromised account. By flagging such anomalies quickly, AI enables banks to prevent fraudulent transactions before they cause significant damage.

> **Example**
>
> In the field of cybersecurity, AI tools are used to detect anomalies in network traffic or access patterns that might signal a potential security breach. For example, AI can identify sudden spikes in traffic or unexpected access to sensitive systems, enabling early detection of attacks. By catching these anomalies early, organizations can respond swiftly to mitigate risks such as data breaches or system down
>
> Overall, AI's ability to detect anomalies plays a crucial role in helping organizations quickly identify potential threats and minimize risks. Whether in financial services or cybersecurity, AI systems enable faster response times and more efficient threat management.

Discovering Hidden Insights

AI has a remarkable ability to discover hidden insights—patterns or relationships that are often too subtle or complex for humans to notice on their own. These insights go beyond obvious trends or clear anomalies, revealing important information that might otherwise stay unnoticed. This skill is especially valuable today, as businesses face huge volumes of data.

Many hidden insights lie within unstructured data such as text, images, or customer reviews—types of information that traditional analytics tools struggle to handle. While structured data like sales numbers or demographics is easier to analyze, unstructured data holds rich, valuable details that are harder to extract. For instance, customer reviews might include feedback on product quality, sentiments about service, or clues about emerging trends—all difficult to measure without advanced AI methods.

Modern AI technologies like natural language processing (NLP) and deep learning allow systems to analyze and interpret this unstructured data. NLP helps AI grasp the sentiment, tone, and context within text, whether it's from product reviews, social media posts, or customer interactions. Deep learning is especially useful for processing images and videos, enabling AI to spot patterns or features that humans might miss.

By combining these techniques, AI can uncover insights across various types of data—patterns that might be hidden in plain sight. For example, AI could analyze customer feedback to detect subtle product issues that many users overlook or spot emerging social media trends before they become widespread. By processing vast amounts of unstructured data and understanding its deeper meaning, AI helps businesses make smarter decisions and stay ahead in a competitive landscape.

Example

A company conducting sentiment analysis on customer reviews might discover that while a new product is generally rated highly, there is a recurring complaint about packaging inconvenience. This kind of insight could easily be buried under overall positive feedback but, once detected, can lead to targeted improvements that enhance customer satisfaction.

Review Questions

1. What role does AI play in finding patterns in data?
2. How does AI help find relationships between things in data?
3. What is AI's role in detecting unusual data (anomalies)?
4. How does AI find insights that people might not see on their own?

7-3 Real Time Decision Making

Real-time analytics refers to the process of analyzing data as it is created or received. AI plays a crucial role in this by processing incoming data streams instantly to make immediate decisions. Unlike traditional batch processing, which analyzes data after it has been collected, real-time analytics enables businesses to act on data immediately, improving decision-making speed and responsiveness.

Learning Outcomes

Learning Outcomes
7-3-1 Define real-time analytics and distinguish it from batch processing.
7-3-2 Understand how AI enables real-time decision-making through data analysis.
7-3-3 Describe key technologies behind real-time analytics.
7-3-4 Recognize real-world applications of AI in real-time decision-making.
7-3-5 Assess the benefits of real-time analytics for businesses.

How AI Powers Real-Time Analytics

AI systems use machine learning algorithms to analyze data as it arrives, enabling quick decisions without needing human intervention. These systems continuously monitor incoming data streams, spotting important patterns, trends, or unusual activity almost instantly—often within milliseconds. This real-time analysis helps businesses respond immediately to changing situations, giving them a competitive advantage.

One of AI's biggest strengths in real-time analytics is its ability to process huge amounts of data very quickly. Traditional analysis methods can slow down when faced with large datasets, but AI can keep up, allowing faster and more accurate decision-making. AI tools also learn from past data and adjust to new information over time, improving their predictions and accuracy.

For example, in fraud detection, AI examines financial transactions as they happen, constantly searching for suspicious patterns. By identifying these irregularities right away, AI can flag potentially fraudulent transactions before they're completed, reducing losses and protecting customers. This speed and precision would be difficult to achieve with manual checks, where delays might let fraud slip through.

In e-commerce, AI can instantly analyze what a customer is browsing, how long they spend on pages, and their purchase history. Based on this, AI can offer real-time product recommendations, helping businesses boost sales and improve the shopping experience. This example shows how AI uses live data to guide business decisions, personalizing customer interactions and driving growth.

Overall, AI's ability to process and act on data in real time is changing how organizations operate. It helps them anticipate customer needs, detect risks early, and streamline operations for better results. Whether it's catching fraud, suggesting products, or adapting to market shifts, AI's real-time power adds significant value across many industries.

Technologies Used

AI-powered real-time analytics relies on several advanced technologies that enable systems to process and analyze data instantaneously. These technologies allow AI to recognize patterns, detect anomalies, and make real-time decisions, improving the speed and accuracy of business operations across various industries. By leveraging machine learning, stream processing, edge computing, and more, AI systems can analyze vast amounts of data quickly and efficiently. Below, we explore the key technologies that power AI-driven real-time analytics.

Real Time Analytics Technologies

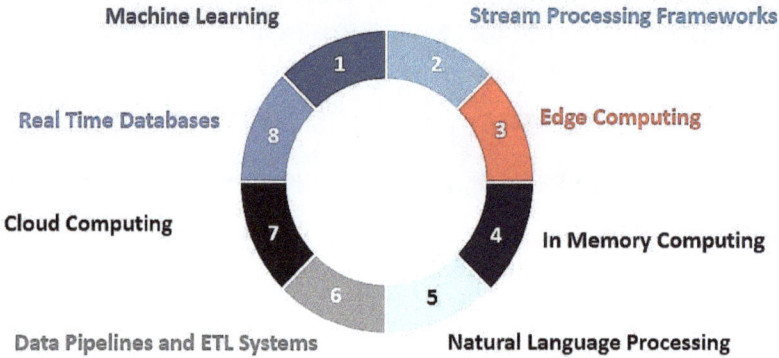

Machine Learning   Stream Processing Frameworks

Real Time Databases   Edge Computing

Cloud Computing   In Memory Computing

Data Pipelines and ETL Systems   Natural Language Processing

Machine Learning Algorithms

At the core of AI-powered real-time analytics are machine learning (ML) algorithms. These algorithms are designed to learn from historical data and identify patterns, making them ideal for real-time decision-making. As new data arrives, AI models can immediately process it, updating their predictions and decisions based on the new information. Common ML techniques such as decision trees, neural networks, and support vector machines are frequently used in real-time applications like fraud detection, recommendation systems, and predictive maintenance. These algorithms continuously adapt to evolving data, making them highly effective at providing real-time insights and driving actionable decisions.

Stream Processing Frameworks

Real-time analytics requires the ability to process data continuously as it is generated. This is where stream processing frameworks come into play. These frameworks are designed to handle high-velocity data and process it in real time, enabling businesses to act on emerging trends or anomalies as they happen. Apache Kafka, for example, is a distributed event streaming platform that allows businesses to collect, process, and store data in real time. Apache Flink, another popular stream processing framework, is designed for applications like financial trading or fraud detection, where every second counts. These tools are crucial for industries that rely on processing large volumes of data quickly and accurately to make decisions on the fly.

Edge Computing

Edge computing is a technology that brings data processing closer to the source of data generation, such as sensors or IoT devices, rather than relying on centralized cloud servers. This reduces latency, making it ideal for applications where real-time decision-making is critical. For example, in autonomous vehicles, edge computing enables AI systems to process sensor data immediately, allowing the vehicle to make decisions in real time, such as avoiding an obstacle. Similarly, in manufacturing, edge devices can monitor equipment and identify potential failures before they occur, reducing downtime and maintenance costs. By processing data locally, edge computing not only speeds up the decision-making process but also reduces the amount of data that needs to be transmitted to central servers, improving efficiency and bandwidth usage.

In-Memory Computing

In-memory computing is another technology that plays a significant role in real-time analytics. It involves storing data in a system's RAM (random access memory) rather than on slower storage devices like hard drives or SSDs. This enables much faster data retrieval and processing speeds, which is essential for applications that require near-instantaneous responses. In-memory computing platforms such as Apache Ignite and MemSQL are optimized to handle real-time analytics, providing businesses with the ability to process large datasets quickly without delays. This technology is particularly useful in applications like fraud detection, dynamic pricing, and customer recommendation engines, where speed is crucial for timely decision-making.

Natural Language Processing (NLP)

Natural language processing (NLP) is an AI technology that enables systems to interpret and understand human language in real time. In real-time analytics, NLP is used to process unstructured data such as customer reviews, social media posts, or support tickets. By analyzing the sentiment, intent, and context behind these texts, AI systems can provide valuable insights into customer behavior, market trends, or potential issues. For instance, a company might use NLP to analyze customer feedback from social media in real time, allowing them to address concerns or capitalize on positive sentiment immediately. Technologies like spaCy, BERT, and GPT are commonly used in NLP for real-time language understanding and analysis.

Data Pipelines and ETL Systems

Data pipelines and ETL (Extract, Transform, Load) systems are essential for efficiently processing and transporting data in real-time analytics environments. These systems continuously collect, clean, and transform data from various sources and load it into databases or AI models for analysis. In real-time scenarios, data pipelines must be able to handle large data streams and process them without delay. Tools like Apache NiFi and AWS Kinesis enable businesses to automate the flow of data, ensuring that information is always up to date and ready for analysis. Real-time data pipelines play a critical role in ensuring that AI systems always work with the most current data, allowing for timely decisions.

Cloud Computing and Serverless Architectures

Cloud computing platforms, such as AWS, Microsoft Azure, and Google Cloud, provide the infrastructure needed to support real-time analytics. These platforms offer scalable resources and on-demand computing power, which is essential for handling the large volumes of data that AI systems process in real time. Serverless computing, a model where users pay only for the resources they use, allows organizations to run real-time analytics applications without having to manage the underlying infrastructure. This makes it easier to scale applications as needed and reduces the cost and complexity of maintaining servers. With cloud computing, AI-driven real-time analytics becomes more accessible and affordable for businesses of all sizes.

Real-Time Databases

Real-time databases are specifically designed to store and process data quickly, allowing for immediate access and analysis. Unlike traditional databases, real-time databases are optimized for low-latency access, which is crucial for applications requiring fast decision-making. Technologies like Redis, Cassandra, and Firebase Realtime Database provide businesses with the ability to retrieve and analyze data instantly, making them ideal for applications like dynamic pricing, live analytics, and real-time recommendation engines.

AI-powered real-time analytics relies on a combination of advanced technologies to process and analyze data instantly, enabling businesses to make fast, informed decisions. By utilizing machine learning, stream processing, edge computing, and other technologies, AI systems can provide real-time insights that improve operational efficiency, customer experiences, and decision-making capabilities. As these technologies continue to evolve, the potential for AI in real-time analytics will only expand, offering even more opportunities for businesses to leverage data for competitive advantage.

Review Questions

1. What is the difference between real-time analytics and batch processing?
2. How do machine learning algorithms support real-time decision-making?
3. Why is stream processing crucial for real-time analytics?
4. How does edge computing improve real-time decision-making?
5. Give an example of how AI-powered real-time analytics can detect fraud.
6. How do cloud computing and serverless architectures help with real-time analytics?

7-4 Optimization and Operations Automation

Optimization and automation are essential factors that boost efficiency in business operations. Optimization means improving systems, resources, and strategies to reach the best possible results—whether that's cutting costs, increasing productivity, or enhancing service quality. Automation uses technology to carry out repetitive tasks without needing human involvement, freeing up people to focus on more strategic work. In data analytics, AI plays a vital role in driving both optimization and automation by analyzing large volumes of data to reveal insights, forecast trends, and suggest actions that make operations smoother. With these abilities, AI helps businesses make quicker, smarter decisions, which leads to better performance and a stronger competitive edge.

Learning Outcomes

7-4-1 Understand how AI optimizes business operations.

7-4-2 Explain how AI automates repetitive tasks to improve efficiency.

7-4-3 Identify real-world examples of AI in optimization and automation.

7-4-4 Recognize the benefits and challenges of using AI in operations.

AI in Data-Driven Optimization

Optimization in business means improving processes to get the best results while using the least amount of resources. AI plays a key role in this kind of data-driven optimization by helping companies make smarter and faster decisions based on large datasets. Whether it's optimizing how resources are allocated, scheduling tasks, or managing logistics, AI boosts efficiency by spotting patterns and trends that would be hard or even impossible for people to find on their own.

One of the main ways AI supports optimization is through its powerful data analysis abilities. By examining vast amounts of information from different sources, AI can make choices that save time and money. For example, AI algorithms can study past sales figures, customer behaviors, and market trends to figure out the most efficient ways to use resources. This might include deciding where to assign staff, how to control inventory levels, or how to plan production schedules.

A strong example of AI-powered optimization is seen in supply chain management. AI can forecast future demand by looking at factors like seasonal patterns, customer habits, and outside influences such as weather or economic shifts. Using these predictions, AI can adjust inventory in real time, helping businesses keep just the right amount of stock. This minimizes waste, avoids running out of products, and improves customer satisfaction by ensuring items are available when needed most.

> **Example**
>
> Walmart is a prime example of how AI can optimize supply chain management. The retail giant uses AI to predict customer demand by analyzing data from various sources, including seasonal trends, consumer behavior, and even weather patterns. By leveraging these insights, Walmart adjusts its inventory levels in real-time, ensuring that stores have the right products in stock without overstocking or running out. This AI-driven approach has helped Walmart reduce waste, prevent stockouts, and improve customer satisfaction by ensuring products are available when customers need them most. As a result, Walmart has enhanced operational efficiency and boosted its ability to respond quickly to market changes.
>
> AI brings a data-driven approach to optimization, helping businesses make more informed decisions, enhance efficiency, and improve overall performance. Whether through better resource allocation, smarter scheduling, or real-time inventory adjustments, AI is becoming an essential tool for modern optimization strategies.

AI in Process Automation

Process automation involves using technology to handle repetitive tasks that would usually require human effort, like entering data, creating reports, or managing customer service. AI plays an important role in making these processes more efficient by applying machine learning and smart algorithms to perform tasks faster, more accurately, and at a larger scale. By using AI, companies can free up employees to focus on higher-value work, while also boosting overall productivity.

One way AI supports automation is through its ability to analyze historical data. AI systems learn how to carry out tasks and make decisions without needing ongoing human supervision. For example, AI-powered chatbots in customer service can respond to common questions by understanding previous interactions and providing helpful answers, reducing the workload for human agents. Likewise, in data management, AI can automate data entry by recognizing patterns in past records and inputting new information quickly and without mistakes.

A strong example of AI-driven automation is automated reporting tools. These systems gather and analyze data from different sources, interpret the results, and produce reports with insights—all automatically. In finance, for instance, AI can pull real-time data from multiple channels, calculate important metrics, and generate reports that highlight financial trends, risks, or opportunities. This speeds up reporting, reduces errors, and allows reports to be customized to fit specific requirements.

> **Example**
>
> JPMorgan Chase, one of the largest financial institutions in the world, has leveraged AI to automate a variety of processes, including financial reporting. The company uses AI-powered systems to automatically gather data from different financial sources, analyze it, and generate reports on key financial metrics, risks, and trends without human intervention.
>
> A notable application is JPMorgan's COiN (Contract Intelligence) platform, which uses machine learning to automate the analysis of legal documents. This system processes thousands of contracts in minutes, a task that would typically take teams of lawyers weeks to complete. In addition, JPMorgan employs AI to automate the generation of financial reports, pulling real-time data from various sources to create insights into the bank's performance. This automation not only speeds up the process but also reduces errors and ensures that reports are tailored to the bank's specific needs.
>
> By implementing AI in process automation, JPMorgan Chase has saved significant time, reduced manual labor, and improved the accuracy of its financial reporting. This allows the company to make quicker, data-driven decisions while reducing operational costs.

AI in process automation is transforming businesses by taking over time-consuming and repetitive tasks, freeing up human workers for higher-value activities. Through data analytics, AI systems can automate tasks like reporting and customer service, improving accuracy, efficiency, and scalability across various industries. This shift is allowing businesses to streamline operations, reduce costs, and increase productivity.

Benefits and Challenges

Benefits and Challenges of AI
in Optimization and Automation

Benefits	Challenges
• Faster decision making • Greater efficiency • Cost savings	• Data quality • Job displacement • Human oversight

AI in optimization and automation brings significant benefits to businesses by enhancing decision-making, improving efficiency, and driving cost savings. One of the primary advantages is faster decision-making. With AI analyzing large amounts of data in real-time, businesses can make more informed decisions quicker, allowing them to respond to market changes, customer needs, and internal challenges much faster than traditional methods. This reduced human error also improves the accuracy of decision-making, as AI systems are less prone to mistakes compared to manual processes.

AI also enhances efficiency in operations and resource use. By automating repetitive tasks like data entry or report generation, businesses can free up valuable human resources for more strategic work. This leads to cost savings by reducing the need for manual labor and improving the productivity of existing staff. Additionally, AI helps optimize resource allocation, such as predicting demand or managing inventory levels, ensuring that resources are used most effectively, which further reduces waste and enhances service delivery.

However, while AI offers many advantages, there are several challenges and considerations that businesses must address. Data quality and accuracy are crucial for AI to function properly—AI systems are only as good as the data they are trained on. Poor data can lead to flawed insights and decisions. Additionally, the growing use of AI for automation raises ethical concerns, particularly around job displacement. As AI takes over tasks previously performed by humans, there is concern about the impact on employment, especially for roles in customer service, manufacturing, and data entry. Finally, despite its capabilities, AI systems should not operate without human oversight, particularly in critical processes. Ensuring that humans remain involved in decision-making for important or sensitive tasks can help prevent AI errors from escalating and maintain accountability.

AI-driven optimization and automation offer clear benefits like faster decision-making, greater efficiency, and cost savings. However, businesses must also address challenges related to data quality, job displacement, and the need for human oversight to ensure responsible and effective use of AI in their operations.

Review Questions

1. How does AI optimize business operations?
2. What tasks does AI automate to improve efficiency?
3. Give an example of AI used in supply chain management.
4. What are the benefits of AI-driven optimization and automation?
5. What challenges do businesses face when implementing AI for operations?

Chapter 8

Bias, Ethics and Laws

8-1 The Issue of Bias

What is Bias?

Bias is an important concept in statistics and data science, referring to a consistent error that causes results to be inaccurate or misleading. It can take different forms depending on the situation, but fundamentally, bias means something is skewed—whether it's how data is gathered, measured, or modeled—and this skew doesn't even out over time. Instead, it pushes results away from the true values in a particular direction.

In statistical estimation, bias occurs when the approach used to calculate a value repeatedly produces results that are systematically too high or too low compared to the actual number. For example, if a researcher tries to find the average height of students but only samples the basketball team, the estimated average will likely be higher than the true average because basketball players tend to be taller. Even if the process is repeated, the flawed sampling method will keep generating skewed results.

Bias is also a key factor in machine learning, especially in the bias-variance tradeoff. Here, bias describes how well a model can capture the real patterns in data. A model with high bias is too simple—it might assume the relationship is a straight line when the data is actually more complex. This leads to underfitting, where the model misses important details. Conversely, low bias suggests the model is more flexible and can learn better from the data. Striking a balance between bias and variance is essential to creating models that predict accurately.

Beyond mathematical bias, there is also algorithmic or social bias. This happens when AI systems or data-driven decisions produce unfair results because of biased training data or built-in assumptions. For instance, a hiring algorithm trained mainly on male resumes might unintentionally favor male applicants. This kind of bias has real consequences, raising important questions about fairness, ethics, and responsibility in technology.

Bias can also emerge in surveys and sampling when the data collected doesn't represent the entire population. If certain groups are excluded or if respondents answer dishonestly due to question wording, the findings won't reflect reality accurately. This issue, known as selection bias or response bias, can undermine the reliability of a study's conclusions.

Overall, bias reminds us that our tools for understanding data—whether simple averages or complex algorithms—are only as effective as the assumptions and methods behind them. Being aware of and addressing bias is vital to producing trustworthy, fair, and useful insights from data.

Types of Bias

Bias in artificial intelligence (AI) and data analytics specifically refers to systematic errors that lead to unfair or skewed outcomes. These biases often stem from the data used to train AI models or algorithms themselves. Bias in AI can manifest in various ways, including:

Sampling Bias

Sampling bias occurs when the training data does not represent the entire population, leading to models that favor certain groups over others. For example, if a facial recognition system is trained primarily on images of light-skinned individuals, it may perform poorly for darker-skinned individuals.

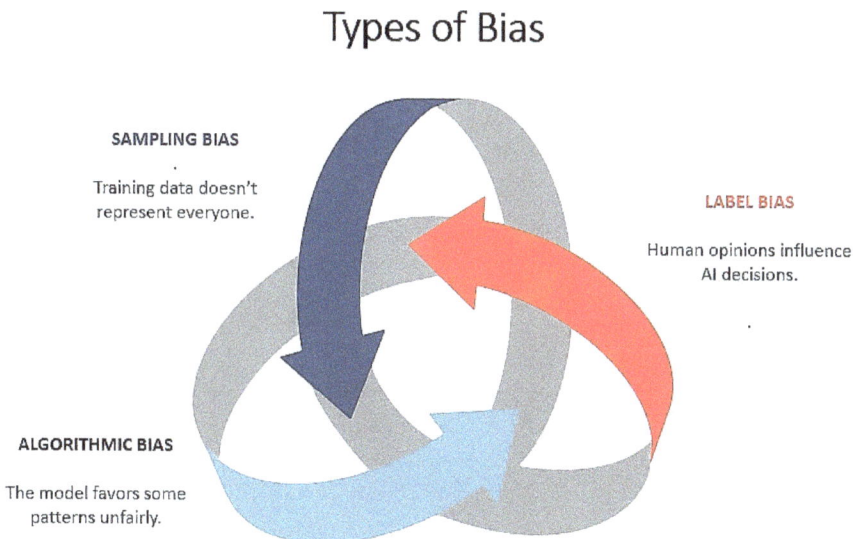

Types of Bias

SAMPLING BIAS

Training data doesn't represent everyone.

LABEL BIAS

Human opinions influence AI decisions.

ALGORITHMIC BIAS

The model favors some patterns unfairly.

Algorithmic Bias

Algorithmic bias arises when the design of an AI model amplifies inequalities present in the data. This can happen if certain features or patterns are unintentionally weighted more heavily, leading to discriminatory predictions. Imagine a company used to mostly hire men, even when women were just as qualified. Now they use AI to help pick new hires, and they train it using their old hiring data. The AI sees that most of the people hired before were men, so it starts to think that men are better choices—even though that's not true.

So now, even if a woman has a great resume, the AI might score her lower just because she doesn't fit the pattern it learned. That's algorithmic bias: the AI picks up unfair patterns from the past and keeps using them in the present.

Label Bias

Label bias happens when people give labels to data based on their own opinions, beliefs, or cultural norms, instead of facts. For example, if a group of reviewers is labeling online comments as "toxic" or "safe," their decisions might reflect personal views—what one person sees as offensive, another might not. If those labels are biased, the AI model trained on them will learn those same biases. That means the AI might wrongly flag certain types of comments or unfairly favor others, just because the original labels weren't neutral or consistent.

Sources of Bias in Data Analytics

Bias in AI doesn't happen by accident—it often comes from deeper issues in how data is collected, labeled, and used during model training. These biases can shape how AI systems behave and lead to unfair or inaccurate outcomes.

One major source of bias is historical inequality in datasets. Many datasets reflect past social or institutional discrimination. For instance, a hiring dataset may show a pattern of favoring certain demographics if previous hiring practices were biased. When AI models learn from this kind of data, they risk repeating the same unfair patterns.

Another source is human subjectivity in data labeling AI often depends on humans to label data, like identifying whether a comment is offensive or safe. But these decisions can be influenced by personal opinions or cultural norms. If the labels are biased, the AI will learn and repeat those judgments.

Finally, flaws in the model training process can also introduce or worsen bias. If the data is unbalanced or if the model doesn't adjust for existing issues, it may overfit to biased patterns or ignore underrepresented groups.

Example

Imagine a bank is using an AI model to decide who should be approved for a loan.

Historical Bias: The data used to train the model comes from past loan decisions. If the bank previously denied more loans to people from certain neighborhoods due to outdated practices, the AI will learn to do the same—even if applicants from those areas now meet all the requirements.

Labeling Bias: Suppose the training data includes notes labeled by loan officers as "risky" or "safe." These labels are subjective and may reflect the personal views of the officers, not actual risk. If they were biased, the AI will pick up on that.

Training Bias: If the data includes far more examples from one group (e.g., high-income individuals), the model may not learn well how to assess lower-income applicants. It may ignore their patterns or misjudge them, leading to unfair denials.

Consequences of Biased AI Models

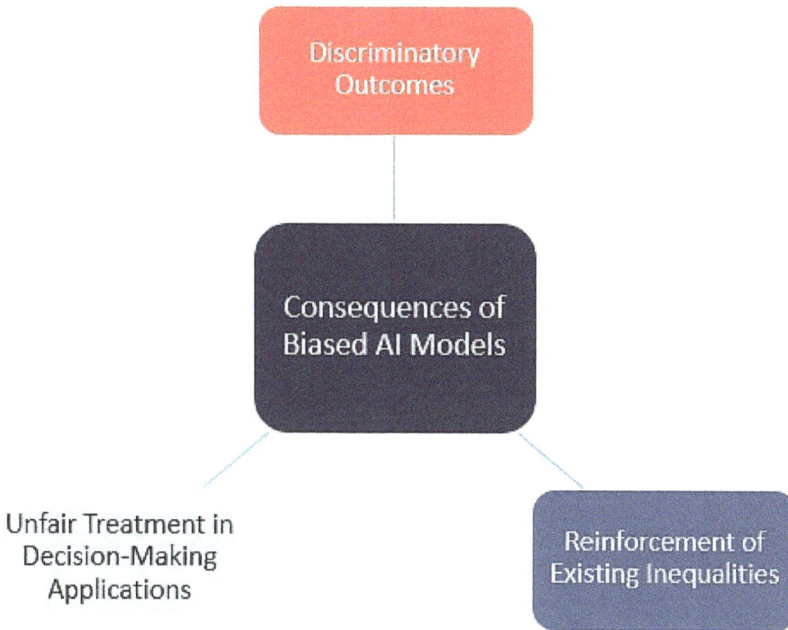

Bias in AI models can have serious and far-reaching consequences, especially when these systems are used in high-stakes areas like hiring, lending, law enforcement, and healthcare. When AI systems are not carefully designed and monitored, they can produce outcomes that are not only inaccurate but also unfair and harmful.

One of the most concerning effects of bias is the risk of discriminatory outcomes. AI models may unintentionally favor certain groups while disadvantaging others, leading to unfair treatment. For example, a biased hiring algorithm might prefer candidates of a particular gender or background, or a credit scoring system might offer better loan terms to one demographic over another. These patterns are not always obvious but can have a lasting impact on people's lives.

Another major consequence is the reinforcement of existing inequalities. Many AI systems are trained on historical data that reflects past biases—such as racial disparities in arrest records or employment practices. Instead of correcting these injustices, biased models often repeat them, further entrenching social and economic divides.

AI is also used in many decision-making processes that affect people's opportunities and well-being. From screening job applications to approving insurance claims, these systems hold real power. If the models are biased, they can make unfair decisions that go unnoticed and unchallenged, especially when their workings are not transparent.

In all these cases, the consequences of AI bias are not just technical—they are ethical and societal. Ensuring fairness in AI is essential to building systems that serve everyone equitably and responsibly.

Strategies to Mitigate Bias

Addressing bias in AI models requires intentional, ongoing efforts to promote fairness, accuracy, and transparency. Without careful attention, AI systems can reinforce existing inequalities or make unfair decisions. Below are some key strategies used to reduce bias and build more trustworthy AI.

Ensuring Diverse and Representative Datasets

One of the most important steps is to train AI models on data that reflects a broad and balanced range of people, experiences, and situations. When datasets include voices and perspectives from different demographic groups, the model is less likely to favor one group over another. This helps reduce sampling bias and makes predictions fairer.

Regular Bias Audits and Fairness Testing

AI systems should be tested regularly to check for biased behavior. This includes running fairness tests, conducting bias audits, and assessing the real-world impact of the model. These evaluations help catch problems early and provide an opportunity to adjust the model before it causes harm.

Developing Explainable AI (XAI) Models

Explainable AI focuses on building models that people can understand and interpret. When users and developers can see why a model made a certain decision, it becomes easier to spot unfair patterns and correct them. Transparency also helps build trust in AI systems and supports accountability.

By combining these strategies, developers and organizations can create AI that is not only powerful but also responsible and fair.

Review Questions

1. What is bias in AI?
2. What are some types of bias in AI?
3. How can past data cause bias in AI?
4. How do human labels affect AI?
5. What problems can biased AI cause?
6. How can we reduce bias in AI?
7. Why is Explainable AI important?
8. Why is fairness important in AI?

8-2 Data Privacy and Security

Learning Outcomes

8-2-1 Understand the difference between ethics and law in data and AI.

8-2-2 Know why data privacy is important.

8-2-3 Identify risks to privacy in AI, like data breaches and re-identification.

8-2-4 Learn ways to protect data privacy, such as encryption and transparency.

Ethics in data and AI refers to the moral principles guiding how data is collected, used, and protected, as well as how AI systems are designed and deployed. It focuses on ensuring fairness, transparency, accountability, and respect for privacy. For example, ethical considerations in AI might include avoiding bias in algorithms, ensuring informed consent for data use, and promoting equal treatment of all users.

Ethics vs Law

Ethics vs Law in Data and AI

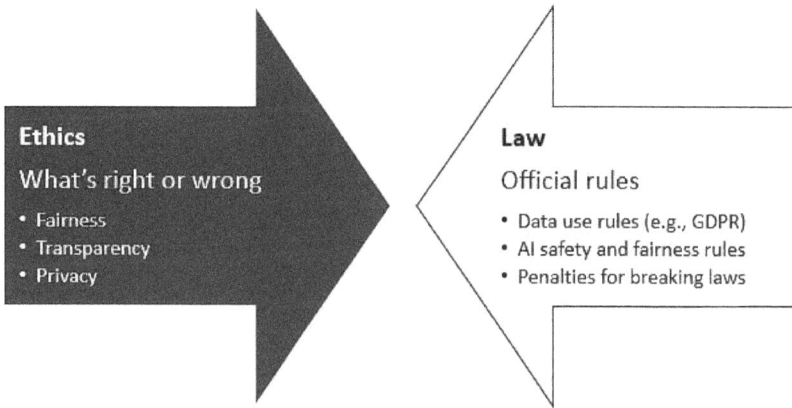

Ethics
What's right or wrong
- Fairness
- Transparency
- Privacy

Law
Official rules
- Data use rules (e.g., GDPR)
- AI safety and fairness rules
- Penalties for breaking laws

Law, in the context of data and AI, refers to the legal rules and regulations that govern how data can be collected, processed, and protected, as well as how AI technologies can be developed and used. Laws like the GDPR (General Data Protection Regulation) set out clear rules on data protection, while laws may also regulate AI for safety, discrimination, and accountability. Legal frameworks are enforceable and violating them can lead to penalties or lawsuits.

In short, ethics is about what is morally right and fair, while law is about what is legally required and enforceable. Ethics often guide decisions where the law may be silent or unclear, and the law enforcers standards that must be followed to protect rights and ensure justice.

Data Privacy

Data privacy is a critical ethical issue that revolves around protecting individuals' personal information and ensuring it is used responsibly. Organizations must respect people's right to control their own data, avoid misuse, and be transparent about how data is collected, stored, and shared. Failing to protect data privacy can lead to harm, exploitation, or loss of trust, which makes it a significant ethical concern in today's digital age.

As organizations increasingly rely on data to make decisions, safeguarding user privacy has become essential. Proper data privacy ensures that personal information is handled responsibly, preventing misuse and unauthorized access. Without adequate safeguards, AI systems can jeopardize sensitive data, creating both ethical and legal challenges.

Risks Associated with AI and Data Privacy

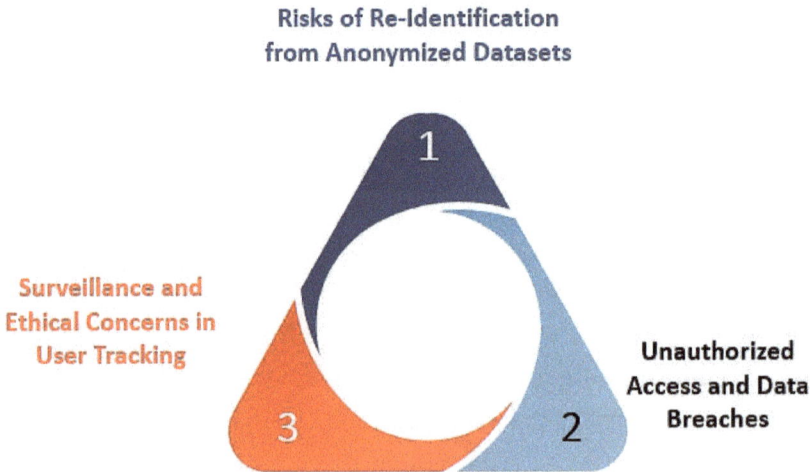

Risk Associated with Data Privacy

Risks of Re-Identification from Anonymized Datasets

1

Surveillance and Ethical Concerns in User Tracking

3

Unauthorized Access and Data Breaches

2

AI systems often depend on vast amounts of data, including personally identifiable information (PII), to make decisions and generate insights. While these capabilities are powerful, they also carry serious risks for data privacy if not carefully managed. One major concern is unauthorized access and data breaches. Cyberattacks, weak security measures, or lapses in data protection can expose sensitive information, leading to issues like identity theft, financial fraud, and harm to the reputations of both individuals and organizations.

Another significant risk involves re-identification from anonymized datasets. Even when efforts are made to anonymize data to protect privacy, advanced AI techniques can sometimes connect different pieces of information to identify individuals again. This raises questions about how effective anonymization methods truly are and poses a serious privacy challenge.

Additionally, AI-driven analytics allow organizations to track and profile users in many ways—through online activity, location data, and facial recognition, among others. While these capabilities can improve user experience and offer personalized services, they also bring ethical concerns. Surveillance, whether obvious or subtle, can infringe on privacy rights and often happens without full informed consent. This creates a difficult balance between technological progress and the protection of individual privacy.

In short, although AI offers tremendous potential, it also introduces important risks to data privacy. Issues like unauthorized data access, re-identification of supposedly anonymous information, and invasive tracking must be carefully addressed to ensure AI technologies are used responsibly and with respect for user privacy.

Best Practices for Ensuring Data Privacy

Protecting data privacy is a crucial responsibility for organizations that manage sensitive information. As concerns about data breaches and privacy grow, companies must take strong measures to secure data and comply with legal requirements. Several key practices can help organizations safeguard privacy while building trust with their users.

One important approach is encryption combined with secure data storage. Encryption scrambles data so that unauthorized individuals cannot read it. This means even if attackers access the data, they cannot understand it. Securing cloud storage and carefully controlling who can access sensitive information further strengthens privacy protections. These steps reduce the chances of unauthorized use and data leaks.

Another critical practice involves data minimization and anonymization. Organizations should limit their data collection to only what is truly necessary for their purposes, reducing the amount of personal information at risk. Anonymizing personal data helps protect user identities by removing identifying details, so even if data is exposed, it cannot be easily traced back to individuals.

Transparency is also vital in maintaining privacy. Companies need to clearly explain to users how their data is collected, processed, and used. Being open about these policies allows users to make informed choices about sharing their information and builds confidence that their privacy is respected.

By implementing measures like encryption, minimizing data collection, anonymizing sensitive information, and maintaining transparency, organizations can better protect user privacy, meet regulatory standards, and foster responsible data management.

Review Questions

1. What's the difference between ethics and law in data and AI?
2. Why is data privacy important?
3. What are two risks to privacy in AI systems?
4. How does encryption protect data?
5. Why should we minimize data collection, and how does anonymization help privacy?
6. What is transparency, and why is it important for data privacy?
7. How can AI cause concerns about surveillance?
8. Name some ways to protect data privacy.

8-3 Laws

Learning Outcomes

8-3-1 Identify key data protection laws (e.g., GDPR, CCPA, AI Act).

8-3-2 Explain why data protection laws are important for privacy and ethical AI.

8-3-3 Describe compliance requirements for data analytics professionals.

8-3-4 Understand challenges in following laws across regions and balancing innovation with ethics.

Major Data Protection Laws

As the digital world grows, governments around the globe have recognized the need to protect individuals' privacy and promote ethical practices in the development and use of AI. Several significant data protection laws have been put into place to ensure that personal data is handled responsibly and that AI technologies are deployed in ways that respect individual rights.

Here, we explore some of the most important regulations designed to safeguard privacy and ethical AI practices.

One of the most comprehensive and strict data protection regulations is the General Data Protection Regulation (GDPR) in the European Union. Enforced in 2018, the GDPR has set a high standard for data protection worldwide. It mandates that organizations must obtain clear and informed consent from individuals before collecting personal data. In addition, it grants individuals the right to access, correct, and delete their data. This regulation also requires organizations to provide individuals with transparency about how their data is used and to notify them in case of data breaches. GDPR places heavy fines on organizations that fail to comply, thus encouraging them to adopt robust data protection practices.

In the United States, California Consumer Privacy Act (CCPA) is another significant law that enhances privacy rights. Introduced in 2020, the CCPA provides California residents with greater control over their personal data. The law ensures that individuals have the right to know what data is being collected about them and the purpose of its use. Additionally, the CCPA gives individuals the ability to opt out of the sale of their personal data, empowering them to protect their privacy. Businesses that fail to comply with the CCPA can face significant penalties, making it crucial for organizations to be transparent and respect consumers' rights.

As AI continues to advance, new regulatory frameworks are emerging to address the ethical and legal challenges posed by this technology. One such example is the AI Act (EU Proposal), which is currently being discussed in the European Union. This proposed regulation aims to establish comprehensive guidelines for the development and deployment of AI systems. The AI Act emphasizes the need for transparency in AI decision-making, fairness in algorithmic outcomes, and accountability for AI systems that impact individuals' lives. The regulation also seeks to address risks associated with high-stakes AI applications, such as those used in healthcare, law enforcement, and hiring processes. While still in the proposal stage, the AI Act represents a proactive approach to regulating AI and ensuring that AI technologies are used in a way that is ethical, transparent, and respects human rights.

These major data protection laws represent significant steps toward safeguarding privacy and ensuring ethical practices in AI. By enforcing consent, transparency, and accountability, these regulations help ensure that individuals' personal data is protected and that AI technologies are developed and deployed responsibly. As technology continues to evolve, it is likely that additional laws and regulations will be introduced to address emerging challenges and further promote ethical AI practices.

Compliance Requirements

As the use of AI and data analytics grows, professionals in these fields must ensure that their work complies with ethical guidelines and legal requirements. Adhering to regulatory frameworks is crucial to protect individuals' privacy, promote fairness, and ensure that data analytics practices are transparent and responsible. Below, we explore some key compliance requirements for data analytics practitioners.

Compliance Requirements for Data Analytics Practitioners

User Consent and Data Transparency	Organizations must obtain explicit consent from users before collecting and processing their data and provide clear information on how data is used.
Right to Explanation in AI-Driven Decisions	GDPR mandates that individuals have the right to understand AI-driven decisions that impact them, such as loan approvals or job applications.
Ethical AI Development Practices	Companies should implement fairness and accountability measures, such as bias testing and impact assessments, to prevent discriminatory AI outcomes.

One of the most important compliance requirements is obtaining user consent and ensuring data transparency. Organizations must secure explicit consent from users before collecting or processing their personal data. This means informing users about the type of data being collected, the purpose for which it will be used, and how it will be processed. Transparency is essential, as it enables users to make informed decisions about whether they want to share their data. Data analytics professionals should ensure that data collection practices are clear, easily understood, and comply with regulations such as the General Data Protection Regulation (GDPR).

Another significant requirement is the right to explanation in AI-driven decisions. Under the GDPR, individuals have the right to receive an explanation when an automated decision is made about them, especially if the decision has significant consequences, such as loan approvals, hiring decisions, or credit scoring. Data analytics practitioners working with AI systems must en-sure that individuals can understand how their data is being used to make decisions and why those decisions are being made. This requirement is par-ticularly important to prevent AI systems from making unfair or biased deci-sions that could impact individuals' lives negatively.

Finally, ethical AI development practices are essential to ensure fairness and accountability in AI systems. Companies should implement measures to test for bias and conduct impact assessments to ensure that their AI systems do not produce discriminatory or harmful outcomes. This includes examining the data used to train AI models for potential biases and making adjust-ments to reduce them. Ethical practices also involve considering the long-term social impact of AI systems, ensuring that these technologies promote fairness and respect for human rights. Data analytics professionals must be proactive in adopting ethical standards and ensuring that their work aligns with both legal regulations and broader societal values.

Compliance with legal and ethical standards is crucial for data analytics practitioners. By ensuring user consent, providing transparency in AI-driven decisions, and following ethical AI development practices, professionals can help foster trust in AI technologies and protect individuals' rights. These compliance requirements not only safeguard privacy but also contribute to the responsible and fair use of AI in data analytics.

Challenges

Data protection laws serve as a vital framework for ensuring the responsi-ble development and deployment of artificial intelligence (AI). These laws aim to safeguard individuals' privacy, promote transparency, and prevent discriminatory practices in AI. However, despite the progress made, several challenges persist in the application of data protection laws, especially in the context of AI development. Two of the most prominent challenges are the varying regulations across regions and the need to balance innovation with ethical responsibility.

One significant challenge is the variation in regulations across different regions. While data protection laws like the General Data Protection Regulation (GDPR) in Europe have set high standards for privacy and AI governance, other countries have adopted different approaches to data protection, or in some cases, lack comprehensive privacy laws altogether. For instance, the United States has a fragmented regulatory landscape, with individual states like California implementing their own privacy laws, such as the California Consumer Privacy Act (CCPA). This creates difficulties for global organizations that operate across multiple jurisdictions, as they must navigate and comply with a patchwork of laws. Ensuring full compliance with these regulations can be a logistical challenge, especially when companies must adapt their AI systems to meet the specific requirements of each region while maintaining efficiency and effectiveness in their operations.

Challenges in Implementing Legal Compliance in AI

Regulatory Variation Across Regions	Different countries have different data protection laws
	Examples: GDPR (Europe), CCPA (California, USA)
	Difficulties for companies to comply with inconsistent regulations
Balancing Innovation and Ethics	Need to drive AI innovation while respecting privacy and fairness
	Ethical concerns: bias, accountability, data misuse
	Tension between business goals and social responsibility
Rapid AI Development vs. Slow Regulation	Laws often lag behind technology
	Regulatory frameworks struggle to keep up with new risks and uses

The second major challenge is balancing innovation with ethical responsibility. AI holds immense potential for business growth and technological advancement, but it also raises significant ethical concerns, particularly around privacy, fairness, and accountability. As organizations strive to leverage AI for competitive advantage, they must ensure that their innovations do not compromise ethical standards or violate data protection laws. This balance is often difficult to achieve. On one hand, businesses are under pressure to develop cutting-edge AI technologies that drive profitability and enhance customer experiences. On the other hand, they must also adhere to ethical guidelines that prioritize consumer protection, privacy, and fairness. For example, AI systems that use personal data to predict consumer behavior or offer personalized recommendations must be designed in a way that respects individuals' privacy and avoids bias or discrimination. Striking this balance requires careful consideration of both legal obligations and broader social responsibility.

Moreover, the rapid pace of AI innovation further complicates the regulatory landscape. Laws and regulations tend to lag behind technological advancements, making it challenging for legislators to craft policies that effectively address emerging risks and opportunities in AI. As AI technologies evolve, regulators must adapt their frameworks to ensure they continue to protect individuals' rights while fostering an environment where innovation can flourish.

While data protection laws are essential for promoting responsible AI development, several challenges remain. The differences in regulations across regions and the need to balance innovation with ethical responsibility create complex hurdles for organizations seeking to comply with legal frameworks and maintain ethical standards. To address these challenges, policymakers must continue to collaborate with industry stakeholders to create more harmonized global regulations and provide clearer guidance on how businesses can innovate while respecting privacy and promoting fairness. By doing so, they can help ensure that AI continues to be developed and deployed in a way that benefits society as a whole.

Review Questions

1. What is the purpose of the GDPR, and how does it affect data practices?
2. What rights does the CCPA give to California residents about their data?
3. What does the AI Act aim to do for AI systems?
4. Why is getting user consent important in data analytics?
5. What is the 'right to explanation' in AI decisions?
6. What challenges do companies face with different data protection laws?
7. Why is it hard for companies to balance innovation and ethical responsibility?
8. What can happen if companies don't follow data protection laws?
9. How can AI systems be made fairer and less biased?
10. How do different data laws affect global AI development?

www.ingramcontent.com/pod-product-compliance
Lightning Source LLC
Chambersburg PA
CBHW051837210326
41597CB00033B/5690